MORE RECIPES From A Country Cook

by Bea Toms

Book design by Dick Markey
Front cover and inside color photography by John Keith

ISBN: 0-9743715-7-2

PUBLISHED BY DIVERSIONS PUBLISHERS
FREDERICK, MARYLAND

Printed in the United States

DEDICATION

I dedicate this book to all good cooks who day after day,
provide their families with good, wholesome food.
You are creating pleasant memories for those you love.
The dinner table can be a haven for the weary.
There, we can feed and revitalize our bodies, minds,
hearts and souls. It can truly be a refreshing oasis
in this hectic, busy world in which we live.

My deepest appreciation and thanks
to Richard Markey for his patience, artistry
and craftsmanship in creating the design of this book.
To Linda Markey, my forever thanks
for the endless hours she spent typing these pages.
And to all my friends and family members,
my gratitude and love for inspiring and giving me
confidence along the way,
particularly at this time in my life.

Thank you, thank you,
and may God bless you, one and all.

FOREWORD

I have been cooking most of my ninety-two plus years; from the time I was twelve years old, until the present time. I am still actively engaged in preparing foods for bridal showers, luncheons, christenings, birthday and anniversary parties, picnics and other family functions.

Over the years I have been asked for my recipes and urged to compile them into a cookbook. I feel it is now time to share them with my many friends and anyone who might wish to have them.

Many of my recipes date back to the 1930's and before. Early in my life I lived with a farm family in Frederick County, Maryland. I assisted with the farm chores, and also the cooking. There were always the daily meals to prepare, cooking for butcherings, holiday preparations, and feeding the threshing hands at harvest time. The men worked hard and had large and appreciative appetites. I learned to cook in large quantities, by necessity, on many of these occasions.

At eighteen and one half years, I married my husband, Clarke Toms in 1932. We had been classmates in high school. For a time we lived with his parents on the family farm. My husband's mother, (we were calling her "Grandma" fifteen months later), Grandma Toms, was a good and generous cook, having reared nine children. My husband was her youngest child. Some of my cooking knowledge, I attribute to her expertise and culinary skills, for everything was made from "scratch". On Saturdays, we prepared extra foods, baked pies and cakes in case "company" might drop in on Sunday. Oft times we might invite someone from church to come home with us, or family members or friends might just drop by in the afternoon. There were no fast-food stores or markets to which we might rush in case of an emergency. Friends and families visited one another more back then, after all, there was no television, or football games and country folk were not too well informed about the game of golf.

Several years later we were farming a large dairy farm in Montgomery County, Maryland. A very prominent doctor owned it. I took care of his aged, invalid mother. Frequently I prepared the food and served dinner parties for him and his fellow doctors and other guests. It was quite a challenge for me, but his guests seemed to enjoy and appreciate my foods. It was a great inspiration to me, country cook that I was.

My oldest daughter, Joan, was married while we were there. I prepared the food for her wedding reception, which was held in the doctor's home, in which we lived. People began asking for my recipes and the foods that I had prepared.

Ultimately, we moved to a farm we had purchased in Frederick County, Maryland. Our second daughter, Patricia, was married there, and again, I prepared the food for the wedding reception. Guests again were asking for my recipes and prepared foods and that's how it all began. I didn't start going out to serve parties until 1966, but that's another whole story.

My cookbook contains, for the most part, recipes I have created using a little of this and a little of that and some imagination. Many recipes, I have adjusted or amended to suit the times and circumstances. Most of the recipes are the result of experimentation and concentration on taste and eye appeal.

Other recipes I have received from family members and friends over these many years, some dating back some sixty to seventy years; for example, my Slumgullion Stew, which I remember from my early childhood home. The picture of it simmering on the stove is still vivid in my mind. I have created the recipe from the mental picture of the ingredients and the aroma of it cooking, still in my mind.

My daughter, Patricia, first gave my roll recipe to me some thirty or thirty five years ago. She was a Home Economics teacher at the time. I doubt she would recognize the recipe as it now reads. The same would be true of Grandma Toms' recipe for "Qld-Fashioneded Sugar Cookies".

The most difficult part of putting the book recipes together was reducing and defining the proper quantities of the various ingredients, as I had for years prepared the recipes in much larger quantities. I have tried to keep the recipes relatively simple and easy to prepare. I do hope you will enjoy preparing the foods and that you and your family will find the dishes tasty and to your liking.

As you can see by the recipes they have submitted, my daughters and granddaughters are all good cooks. They appreciate the value and satisfaction of serving their families good and wholesome home-cooked meals. There's nothing quite like sitting around the family table and enjoying a pleasant happy meal together.

Good food is one of life's great pleasures, as well as spending time with those we love. It is a time, precious time, we and our families can spend together creating never-to-be forgotten memories of the wonderful meals and happy times we have shared.

My profound thanks to you and to those of you who have permitted me to share in the happy and special times in the lives of so many of your families. I assure you it has been a very special privilege. Through the years so many have accepted my efforts and made me very happy to feel that, even at my age, I still have something to offer. You have given me a very special gift. Thank you, thank you.

I began writing poetry in my late eighties.
I have had two books of poetry published since then.
This is the first poem I wrote,
and I would like to share it with you.

Speak To Me My Soul

Speak to me my soul,
lead me by your hand.
Let my heart rejoice,
if that is in your plan.
Keep my mind and being,
within God's precious will.
Let me not complain
of life's capricious ways.
We all are here on earth,
for just a few short days.
Help me then, to see the joy,
in all of life, I pray.
That I may help another soul,
along life's rugged way.

Contents

It is just about impossible

to smile on the outside

when one is frowning on the inside.

Appetizers

Open Face Party Sandwich Spread

Open face sandwiches can be made with almost any kind of bread- white, whole wheat, rye, pumpernickel, cinnamon, raisin, date and nut, etc.

The bread may be made into pin-wheels, cut into rounds, squares, rectangles, diamonds, or on colored bread, and so on. The following are recipes for some of the combinations of spreads for the different breads I have used over the years.

WHITE BREAD

cream cheese
deviled ham
minced sweet pickle
minced green or pitted black olives

cream cheese
minced onion or garlic salt
bit of anchovy paste
minced cucumber

CINNAMON OR RAISIN BREAD

cream cheese
pineapple or apricot preserves
finely chopped pecans

cream cheese
finely chopped apples
peach or strawberry jam
finely chopped nuts

RYE BREAD

cream cheese
extra sharp shredded cheese
minced green olives
deviled ham
finely diced hard cooked eggs

cream cheese
Old English cheese spread
minced green or black olives
bits of chopped tomatoes

OTHER COMBINATIONS

cream cheese
watercress chopped
tiny spring onions slices
parmesan cheese

cream cheese
flaked crab meat
minced green pepper
finely chopped hard cooked egg

mayonnaise
finely minced cooked chicken
minced celery
finely minced sweet pickle

mayonnaise or
cream cheese
any assortment of finely diced vegetables

Any or all of these combinations can be attractive as well as delicious and heathful as well as fun to make.

Cucumber Dip

1 large firm cucumber
1 ½ tablespoons minced pimento pepper
¼ cup finely chopped green Bell pepper
¼ cup finely minced spring onions
1 ¼ cup sour cream
1 8-ounce package cream cheese
1 tablespoon anchovy paste
dash garlic salt to taste

Wash cucumber, pare or not as you choose.
If very seedy, remove seeds if you wish.
Dice cucumber into small pieces.
Mix sour cream and cream cheese in mixer.
Add anchovy paste and mix well.
Add pimento, onion, Bell pepper and cucumber.
Season to taste with garlic salt. Mix well and chill.
Serve with fresh vegetables, cauliflower, broccoli,
carrots, celery, etc., or as a dip
for various chips or crackers.
About 3-4 cups

Shrimp Party Spread

8 oz canned or frozen small shrimp
½ cup finely diced cucumber
½ cup finely minced spring onions
8 oz cream cheese
2 tablespoons mayonnaise
2 tablespoons sour cream
¼ cup tomato ketchup
Dash hot sauce (optional)

If using canned shrimp, rinse and cover with ice water about one hour and drain well.
Place shrimp, cucumber, onions in bowl.
Blend together cream cheese, mayonnaise, sour cream, ketchup, and if desired, hot sauce.
Blend well. Mix together shrimp and vegetables.
Toss with dressing. Refrigerate until ready to serve.
Firm crackers or melba toast are an ideal accompaniment.
Makes 2½ cups.

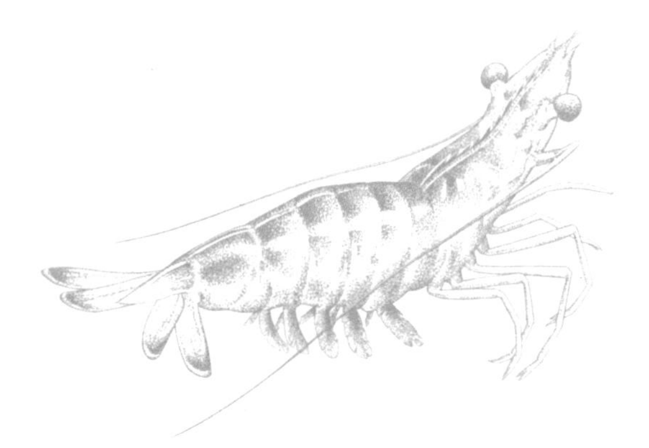

Cocktail Crab-meat Balls

1 pound back fin or special blend crab meat
2 beaten eggs
½ cup fine dry bread crumbs
⅓ cup finely minced green pepper
3 tablespoons melted butter
3 tablespoons flour
½ cup milk
¼ teaspoon salt
Dash Tabasco sauce
Fine dry crumbs (extra)
Frying fat or oil

Pick through crab meat. Remove any shell or cartilage.
Mix together, crab meat, ½ cup bread crumbs, eggs, and green pepper.
Melt butter in saucepan, add flour and stir until well blended.
Slowly add milk, salt and Tabasco sauce. Mix this thick sauce with crab meat, eggs, etc. It acts as a binder to adhere all ingredients together when frying.
If the mixture seems too moist to roll into a ball, add a bit more bread crumbs. If mixture seems too dry to roll, add a bit of milk to mix.
Form mixture into about ¾" balls. Roll them with fine bread crumbs into a firm ball. Place them in a shallow pan or casserole. Cover well and refrigerate several hours or overnight. When ready to fry them, roll them once again to firm them into nice round balls. Fry in hot deep fat. To test temperature of fat, drop one ball in hot fat. If it rises to the surface, the fat is hot enough.
Drop carefully with a large slotted spoon, about 10-15 at a time depending on the diameter of frying pan.
It only takes a few minutes for them to brown.
Remove with the large slotted spoon and drain on paper towels.
Repeat process until all are fried. Keep hot until serving or place them in a flat pan or casserole to be heated at serving time.
Makes about 55-60 (¾") crab balls.
A good cocktail sauce is a good accompaniment at serving time.

(see photo page 33)

Pastry-Covered Sausages

Any small sausages
Vienna sausages
small breakfast sausages
frankfurters
mustard or ketchup
1 double recipe for pie dough (refer to dough recipe, page 174)

Roll half the pie dough into a square.
Frankfurters may need to be cut into halves or thirds, lengthwise.
Cut the rolled pie dough into squares,
slightly wider than the sausage is long.
Place the sausage on one side of the square.
Roll dough and sausage as you would a jelly roll.
Repeat process until all the dough has been used.
Grease or butter lightly a flat jelly-roll type pan.
Place rolled sausages on pan and bake in 450° oven
until dough is browned.
Do not burn. Serve hot.
They are very nice for parties.

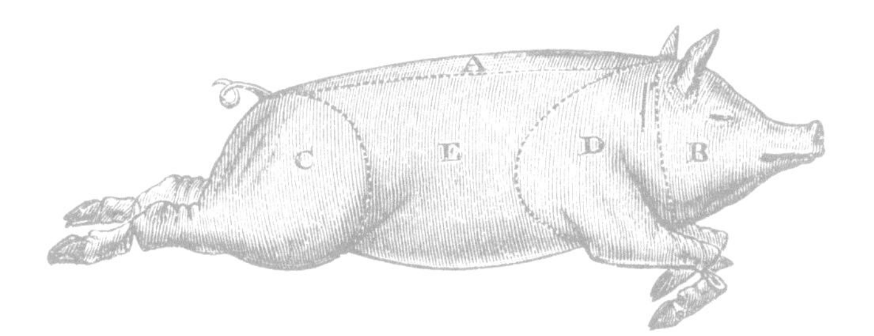

Tiny Cheese Canapés

24 rounds pumpernickel or rye bread
2 (5-ounce) jars Kraft's Old English cheese spread
6 ounces cream cheese
12 pimento-stuffed green olives
Dash of garlic salt

Cut bread rounds with 1¾" cookie or biscuit cutter.
Mix Old English cheese and cream cheese and garlic salt together.
Be sure to have no lumps in spread.
Place a large decorator flower tip in pastry bag.
Fill bag about half full with cheese mixture.
Tighten bag and with a circular motion, form a cheese rose
on each round of bread. Cut olives in half, crosswise.
Place half olive, end down, on cheese rose.
Refrigerate in a covered container until serving time.
These canapés are quick and easy to prepare.
Any leftover cheese may be refrigerated to be used later
or spread on a bread round or cracker and give yourself a treat!
Makes 24 canapés

Easy Petits Fours

1 recipe of your favorite white or yellow cake recipe
or 1 box yellow or white cake mix
Cake frosting
Food color

Mix cake according to your favorite cake recipe or cake mix. Pour batter into greased and floured 10½ x 15½ x 1½" jelly roll type pan and bake according to temperature and time for either recipe. Remove cake from oven and turn out onto flat cookie sheet or other flat surface. Allow to cool thoroughly. Prepare a white frosting or color of your choice frosting. When cake is completely cold, apply frosting. I generally place large dollops of frosting over cake and then spread them evenly over surface of cake. A long thin broad-bladed knife is nice to cover and smooth frosting evenly over cake. I sometimes dip the long blade in water and smooth it one last time. Any frosting along sides of cake may be spread evenly over sides and ends of cake to keep it from drying out. When frosting is completely set, cut lengthwise, 1½" in width, long slices the length of the cake. Repeat until cake is used up. You may wish to cut one slice at a time and then cut it into squares, rectangles, or diamond shapes. Place these in flat pan and cover lightly to keep the little cakes from drying out. Using what is left of the frosting or you may need to make another half recipe for decorating the petits fours. Place half the frosting in one bowl and the other half in another bowl. Add coloring, perhaps light green in one bowl and pink in the other or peach in one and a different shade of green in the other. With a little practice, a pastry tube or pastry bag or two and different decorator tips you can decorate these dainty little cakes quite simply or very elaborately.

The petits fours are very impressive at bridal showers, christenings, teas, etc.

Makes about 60

MY FROSTING FOR PETITS FOURS

2 pounds or 7½ cups confectioner's sugar
⅔ cup Crisco shortening
A scant ⅔ cup milk
2 teaspoons vanilla
⅓ teaspoon salt

Beat shortening well. Add sugar and milk alternating and beating well after each addition. Add salt and vanilla. Scrape sides of mixing bowl. If frosting seems too stiff, add a bit more milk to make it a nice consistency to spread.

Deviled Ham Stuffed Tomatoes

1 (4½ ounce) can deviled ham
4 ounces cream cheese (softened)
½ cup grated Swiss cheese
½ teaspoon grated horseradish (optional)
Cherry tomatoes
Tiny sprigs of parsley

Wash cherry tomatoes.
Cut a thin slice from stem end of each tomato.
Scoop out pulp from tomatoes.
This is easily done with a ¼ teaspoon measuring spoon.
Place tomatoes upside down on plate lined with
paper towels to drain.
Mix together deviled ham, cream cheese, Swiss cheese
and horseradish (if using). Set aside to chill.
When filling is chilled and tomatoes are well drained,
fill tomatoes with deviled ham mixture.
Again, a small measuring spoon is ideal for filling tomato cavities.
Top with tiny sprigs of parsley. Refrigerate until serving time.
Makes about 25 stuffed cherry tomatoes.

Ribbon Sandwiches

1 (8¼ x 2¾ inch) unsliced bread
3 (8 ounce) packages cream cheese
3 (4½ ounce) cans deviled ham
Finely minced sweet pickle

Cut bread horizontally in slices, ⅙" or less. One loaf should cut 8-10 slices. Cover bread slices well to keep from drying out. Blend together in mixing bowl cream cheese and deviled ham. Spread one bread slice with ham-cheese mixture. Sprinkle ham spread with pickle. Spread a second slice with ham-cheese mix. Turn it spread side down on pickle. Spread top of slice with the spread and sprinkle with pickle. Spread a third slice with ham spread and place it ham spread side down. Try to place slices evenly over one another. Spread top of third slice with ham mix and sprinkle with pickle. Spread fourth slice with ham mix and place on top of pickle, spread side down. Smooth edges and sides of sandwich. Wrap in a sheet of saran wrap. Place on cookie sheet or jelly roll pan and put in freezer to chill until very firm. Cut sandwich block into 3 equal sections about 2½" wide. Wrap lightly and return to freezer. When chilled to freezing point, cut each section crosswise into about 8 slices. Wrap again, freeze and store. Using the same directions, you may use any spread you may desire, fruit, cheese, or other combinations alternating spread and pickle, cherries, nuts, etc. The spread slices may also be used to make pinwheel sandwiches. Place pickle, cherries or olives at end of slice of spread bread. Roll up and wrap and proceed as with ribbon sandwiches. Cut rolls into about 8 slices. Wrap and freeze. Examples below. Any of the sandwiches are colorful and nice for parties.

SPREADS

Cream cheese	Cream cheese
Deviled ham	Minced or whole maraschino cherries
Sweet or dill pickle	Finely chopped pecans

RYE BREAD

Cream cheese
Grated extra sharp or Old English cheese spread
Green or pitted ripe olives

Soups & Stews

Creamed Corn Soup

2 cups chicken broth
2 cups canned, frozen or fresh sweet corn
½ cup celery (finely minced)
¼ cup parsley (finely minced) or 1 tablespoon parsley flakes
1 tablespoon (finely minced) onion
2 tablespoons butter
2 tablespoons flour
2 cups milk
2 teaspoons sugar
1 teaspoon salt
½ teaspoon celery salt

Pour chicken broth into soup pot.
Add sweet corn, celery, onion and sugar.
Melt butter in a saucepan, add flour, stir until well blended,
add milk slowly, stirring constantly until it thickens.
Combine sauce and corn.
Mix a small portion of the corn mix to the butter, milk sauce.
Blend all together in soup pot.
Add parsley and seasonings to soup; salt, celery salt,
a bit of pepper, if desired.
Blend and simmer until slightly thickened.
Serves 6

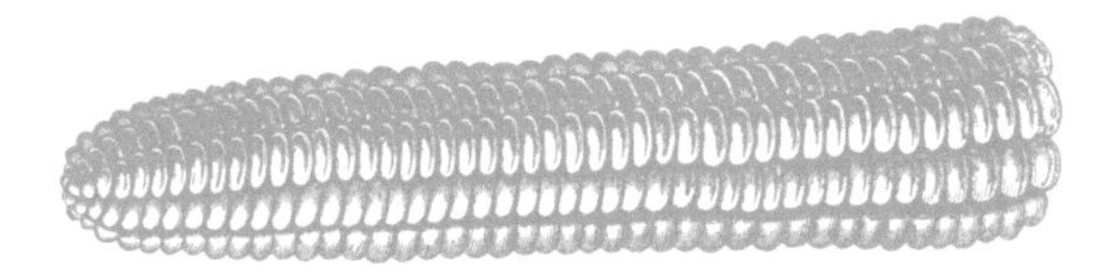

Creamed Green Pea Soup

1 (16-oz.) bag frozen green peas (thawed)
chicken broth or water to cover the peas
¼ cup minced onion
2 teaspoons sugar
1 teaspoon salt
4 tablespoons butter or margarine (melted)
3 tablespoons flour
2 cups half and half milk
dash of celery salt and pepper to taste

Cover the thawed peas with chicken broth or water.
Add the minced onion and sugar.
Bring to a boil and cook slowly until peas are tender.
When the peas, etc. are tender remove from heat.
Drain and save broth.
Run peas and onions through food processor or put both broth and vegetables in blender and blend briefly.
Return all to soup pot.
Put melted butter in a saucepan, add flour, blend well.
Slowly add half and half. Stir all until well blended.
Pour a small amount of the hot peas into the flour, milk sauce, then slowly add and mix together with pea soup.
Simmer, add seasonings.
Stir all well. Serve hot.
Serves 4-6

Super Ham and Corn Bisque

2 cups smoked cooked ham (diced)
1 cup chopped celery
½ cup minced onion
1 stick butter or margarine
2 (16 oz.) cans cream style corn or 4 cups fresh corn with sweet kernals scrapped from cob
1 cup milk
½ teaspoon celery salt
½ teaspoon garlic powder
½ teaspoon pepper
2 teaspoons sugar

In a large sauce pan, sauté the ham, celery and onion in the butter until tender.
Add the corn, milk, celery salt, garlic powder, salt, pepper and sugar.
Bring all to a boil, reduce heat.
Cover and simmer 20-30 minutes. Serve hot.
Hot biscuits on the side are nice.
Garnish with snipped parsley if desired.
Serves 6

What's Its Name Hominy Soup

3 cups chicken or turkey broth
2 cups canned hominy
1½ cups ham, cut in small cubes
½ cup minced onion
½ cup minced celery
½ cup green peas
¼ cup minced Pimento pepper
1 cup cream of chicken or cream of mushroom soup

Pour broth into soup pot.
Add hominy, bring to low boil. Add ham.
The ham should be a mild smoked ham.
Add the rest of ingredients.
Stir in chicken or mushroom soup last.
When all is well blended, reduce heat and
simmer about 45 minutes.
If soup seems too thick add a little chicken broth or milk.
Serves 6

Broccoli Soup

2½ cups chopped broccoli
2½ cups chicken broth
¼ cup chopped onion
3 beaten egg yolks
1½ teaspoons butter
1⅓ cups half and half cream
dash celery salt
salt and pepper to taste

Put broccoli, broth and onion into a saucepan and bring to a boil.
Reduce heat and let it simmer until broccoli is crisp and tender.
Put through a blender.
Return to saucepan and bring to a boil again.
Pour beaten eggs and butter into boiling soup.
Stir vigorously as you slowly pour them. Reduce heat and add in the half and half slowly and stirring all the while.
Season with salt and pepper to taste.
Add a bit more chicken broth if soup seems to be too thick.
Serve hot, garnish with sprigs of parsley if desired.
Serves 4-6

Blackeye Pea Soup

6 cups ham broth. If ham broth is quite salty, use one or two cups of water instead of one or two cups of the ham broth
1 cup peeled, finely diced potatoes
½ cup minced celery
½ cup minced onion
3 cups blackeye peas (fresh cooked or canned, with broth)
½ cup pearl barley
½ cup rivels (optional) *See page 33*
½ tablespoon parsley flakes
dash of pepper

Bring ham broth to boil.
Add all other ingredients except rivels and parsley.
Cook 1-1¼ hours.
Add rivels and parsley in the last 15 minutes of simmering.
Adjust seasoning if desired.
Serves 8-10

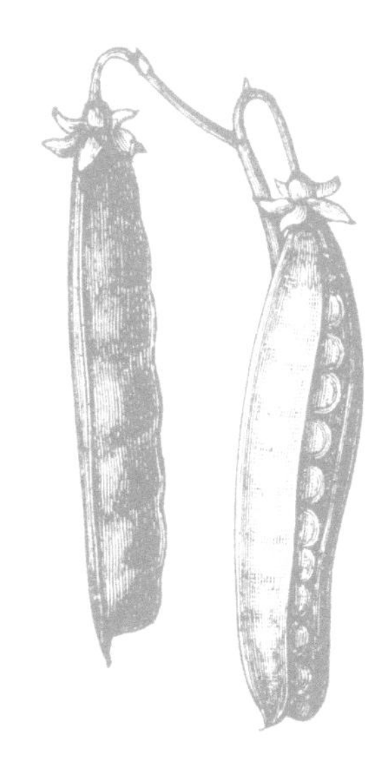

Corn Chowder

5 slices bacon
1 medium onion (finely chopped)
1 small clove of garlic (minced)
1 large rib of celery (finely chopped)
2 cups chicken broth
2 medium size potatoes (peeled and diced)
2½ cups sweet corn (fresh off the cob or frozen or canned)
2 tablespoons flour
2 cups milk
salt and pepper to taste

Sauté the bacon in a skillet.
Remove the bacon to paper towels.
Sauté the onion, garlic and celery in several tablespoons of bacon drippings until just tender.
Crumble the bacon.
Place the sautéed bacon, onions, garlic and celery in chowder pot.
Add chicken broth and potatoes and simmer about 30 minutes.
Gradually add milk to flour and blend together well.
Stir a little of the chowder into the milk-flour blend and then gradually add it to the chowder pot with the rest of the ingredients.
Bring all to boil stage, reduce heat and simmer about 10 minutes or so.
If desired sprinkle with minced parsley and serve.
Serves 6

Cream of Spinach Soup

1 (10 ounce) package frozen chopped spinach
4 cups chicken broth
2 tablespoons butter or margarine
2 tablespoons flour
1 cup hot milk
½ cup sharp Cheddar shredded cheese
Dash of celery salt and pepper to taste
1 tablespoon minced pimento pepper (optional)

Thaw spinach.
Put spinach and one cup chicken broth in blender.
Blend for a few seconds.
Pour into soup pot along with the other three cups of chicken broth.
Bring to boiling point. Melt butter in saucepan.
Add flour and stir until well blended.
Slowly add hot milk and stir until it thickens.
Add to it several tablespoons of the hot spinach and broth.
Slowly stir it back into the soup pot.
Stir and let simmer slowly.
Add celery salt and pepper if desired.
Blend in shredded cheese and simmer about 15 minutes.
Just before serving, add pimento pepper if desired.
Serves 6

Berkeley Springs Cream of Potato Soup

3½ cups ham broth or potato water
3 cups diced potatoes
½ cup carrots, sliced diagonally
1½ cups diced cooked ham
1½cups finely chopped cabbage
½ cup minced onion
Dash celery salt
1½ tablespoons butter, 1½ tablespoons flour, 1½ cups milk (white sauce)

Cook potatoes in lightly salted water.
When done, run potatoes through ricer or mash with potato masher.
Place vegetables and ham in ham broth or potato water.
Cook until tender. Add mashed potatoes to vegetables, etc.
Season with celery salt, salt and pepper to taste.
Simmer until about ready to serve. Make white sauce.
Melt butter in saucepan, add flour, stir until blended, add milk.
Stir until thickened.
Pour a little broth from soup mix into sauce.
Stir and return sauce to simmering soup.
Add a bit of liquid to soup if necessary.
Serves 8-10

Sausage Soup

¾ pound seasoned country sausage
¼ pound hot Italian sausage (highly seasoned)
½ cup minced onion
1 (16-ounce) can tomatoes, chopped
1 tablespoon sugar
1 (24-ounce) can beef or ham broth
2 cups water
2 cups cooked noodles
1 tablespoon minced fresh parsley

Sauté sausage in skillet until lightly browned.
Add onions and sauté briefly. Drain off excess fat, if any.
Add sugar to chopped tomatoes.
Mix together sausage, onions, tomatoes and sugar.
Pour into soup pot. Add beef or ham broth and water.
Simmer all about 15-20 minutes. Increase heat.
Add noodles and cook about 10 minutes until well done.
Add more broth or water if needed to make soup
of the right consistency to serve.
Simmer briefly. Add parsley for garnish.
Serves 6-8

Leftover Turkey or Chicken Soup

4-5 cups turkey or chicken broth
1½ cups cooked and diced turkey or chicken
1 cup diced potatoes
¾ cup finely chopped celery
¼ cup minced onion
½ cup baby carrots, sliced diagonally
⅓ cup minced parsley or 1 tablespoon dried parsley leaves
dash celery salt
rivels (optional, see page 37)

Pour broth into soup pot.
Bring to a boil. Add other vegetables except the parsley.
Bring all to a slow boil. Cut back heat and simmer 35-40 minutes.
Add celery salt. If you plan to use the rivels, bring soup to a boil.
Sprinkle rivels over soup and stir well
to keep them from sticking together.
Sprinkle on parsley.
After several minutes return heat to simmer for several minutes.
Keep hot until serving time.
Makes 6 hearty servings.
Wonderful for a cold winter evening.

Cocktail Crab-Meat Balls

page 15

Beef Barley Soup
page 40

Spinach Bacon Casserole
page 56

Vegetarian Jambolaya

page 60

Rivels

2 cups flour
½ teaspoon salt
1 beaten egg

Mix salt and flour together.
Add beaten egg and mix, either in mixer or
simply rubbing the mixture between the palms of your hands
until it becomes a fine meal.
Sprinkle rivels into boiling soup.
Stir so the rivels do not stick together.
You may not need all the rivels, depending on the amount of liquid
and how thick you wish the soup to be.
Any rivels left over may be frozen and kept to use another day.

Great Northern Bean Soup

4 cups ham broth (use 2 cups ham broth and 2 cups water if ham broth is quite salty)
1 (15½-oz) can Great Northern beans
½ cup finely minced onion
1 cup finely diced potatoes
1 cup diced cooked ham or crisp bacon
1 tablespoon minced pimento pepper (optional)
1 cup fine broken noodles
finely minced parsley for garnish

Pour into soup pot the ham broth or ham broth with one cup of water if broth is too salty. Bring to a boil. Add potatoes and onion. Simmer about 15 minutes. Add beans, bacon or ham, pimento pepper. Simmer on low heat about a half hour. Increase heat and bring to boil. Add and stir in noodles. Boil on low heat until noodles are done. Reduce heat again to simmer. Add any seasonings to soup you may wish. When thoroughly blended and all ingredients are well done, add garnish and serve.

6-8 servings

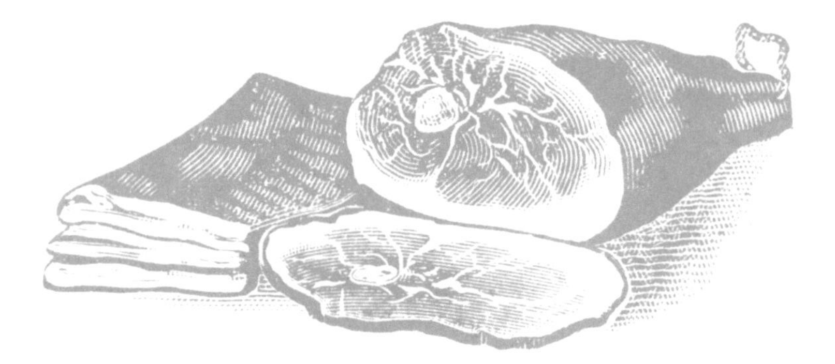

Lentil Soup

1½ cups dry lentils
4 cups chicken or ham broth
½ pound pork sausage or frankfurters
½ cup chopped celery
½ cup minced onion
1 minced clove of garlic
3 tablespoons butter (use 1 tablespoon to sauté meat)
2 tablespoons flour
2 tablespoons catsup
salt and pepper to taste
dash Tabasco sauce

Wash lentils thoroughly and soak in cold water six hour or overnight.
Sauté sausage or frankfurters in one tablespoon of the butter.
Brown nicely, add celery, onion, and garlic.
Pour the 4 cups of broth in the soup pot. Add lentils.
Add sausages or frankfurters. Bring to a boil.
Melt rest of butter in saucepan and add flour.
Stir until well blended.
Put about a half cup of the simmering broth in flour-butter mixture.
Blend well and stir it into soup pot with the meat,
lentils, and other ingredients.
Simmer about 1½ to 2 hours.
Add more broth if necessary.
Serves 8.
A nice green salad is a good accompaniment.

Beef Barley Soup

1 pound stew beef, cut into ½-inch cubes
6-8 cups beef broth or half water, half beef broth
1 tablespoon parsley flakes
1 medium-size onion, minced
1½ cup minced celery
1½ cup thinly sliced carrots
4 oz fine noodles (uncooked)
¾ cup pearl barley
1 cup diced potatoes (optional)
salt and pepper to taste

Dice beef and sauté briefly.
Put into soup pot with broth, parsley, onion, celery and carrots.
Add potatoes and barley. Season with salt and pepper.
Simmer about one-half hour.
Add noodles and continue cooking about another hour
until beef is tender.
Add more broth if necessary.
10 servings

(see photo page 34)

Creole Goulash

5 cups canned red kidney beans
8 slices sautéed and crumbled bacon
4 cups canned tomatoes, chopped
2 teaspoons baking powder
2 tablespoons light brown sugar
2 cups shredded day-or-two old bread
¼ pound grated sharp cheddar cheese
salt and pepper to taste
dash hot pepper sauce (optional)

Remove sautéed bacon from pan.
Crumble and set aside. Add kidney beans to the bacon drippings.
Mix baking powder with chopped tomatoes.
Add brown sugar and salt and pepper or hot pepper sauce to taste.
Pour all into a 9 x 13 x 3" casserole.
Top with grated cheese and then the crumbs that have been lightly buttered and tossed together with the bacon.
The casserole should be covered lightly and baked in a 350° oven about one hour.
You may wish to top with the cheese and then bake about 45 minutes, and then remove casserole from the oven and top with the crumb/bacon mix.
Return casserole to the oven and bake about another 15 minutes or until the bacon and crumb mix is crisp and lightly browned.
The casserole may be made a day ahead if you wish.
Serves 8-10

Oven Beef Stew

1 pound stew beef cut into small cubes
½ cup minced onion
2 tablespoons butter or margarine
2 cups cream of mushroom soup
1 cup water
3 medium-size potatoes, pared and diced
2 medium-size carrots, sliced diagonally
1 cup shredded Cheddar cheese
salt and pepper to taste
flour and a bit of salt to dust beef

Dust beef cubes in flour and a bit of salt.
Sauté beef lightly in butter. Add onion and sauté with beef.
Combine all the rest of the ingredients.
Turn into a buttered casserole and bake
in a 350° oven for 1½ hours.
Keep casserole covered all the time, except to stir
ingredients several times.
Test beef for doneness.
Add another half hour of baking if necessary.
Serves 8

Cream of Crab Soup

2 tablespoons butter
2 tablespoons flour
3 cups heated milk
¼ cup finely minced green or Pimento pepper
¾ tablespoon Worcestershire sauce
1 cup back fin or blend crabmeat
dash Tobasco sauce
½ teaspoon or salt to taste

Check crabmeat for bits of shell or cartilage.
Flake it well. Melt butter in sauce pan. Add flour and blend well.
Add minced green or Pimento pepper. Slowly blend in milk.
Add Worcestershire sauce.
Add dash of Tabasco sauce and salt to taste.
Simmer and stir until well blended. Add crabmeat.
Mix and adjust seasonings to taste.
If mixture is too thick, add enough more milk to thin it
to the right consistency to serve.
Serves 6.

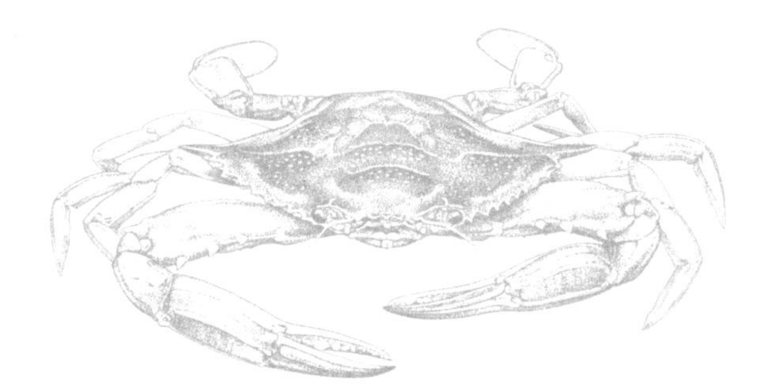

Hope is the food to comfort and sustain us

when we hunger for better days.

Casseroles

Luscious Potato Casserole

4-5 medium size potatoes pared and thinly sliced
1 small clove of garlic (finely minced)
½ stick of butter or margarine (melted)
6 ounces Swiss or Cheddar cheese (shredded)
1 cup milk (bring to boiling point)
salt and pepper to taste

Butter a 1½ to 2 quart baking dish.
Place one half of the potatoes on the bottom of the dish.
Cover lightly with shredded cheese.
Cover with the rest of the potatoes.
Top with the rest of the cheese.
Mix melted butter with hot milk.
Pour down the sides of the casserole so as
not to disturb the cheese topping.
Bake in 375° oven until potatoes are done, about 45 minutes
or until topping is golden.
Cover lightly, if necessary, so as not to burn topping.
Serves 6

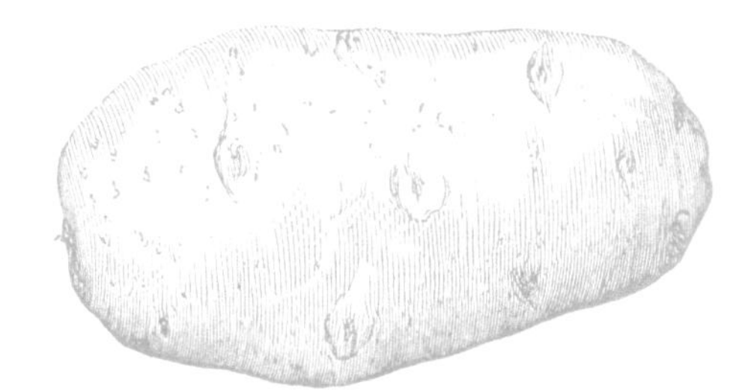

Creamed Broccoli Casserole

1 large head broccoli (cut in small pieces)
2 beaten eggs
1 cup cream of mushroom soup
⅔ cup mayonnaise
2 tablespoons minced onion
⅔ cup shredded Cheddar Cheese
⅔ cup buttered cracker crumbs

There should be about 3½ cups of chopped broccoli.
Cook the broccoli in slightly salted water until slightly crisp.
Remove from heat and drain.
Add mushroom soup to the beaten eggs, mayonnaise
and finely minced onions. Mix all of these ingredients to broccoli.
Pour into buttered casserole.
Mix Cheddar cheese and cracker crumbs together
and spread over casserole.
Bake in 300° oven until casserole is bubbly
and topping is lightly browned.
Serves 4-6

Broccoli Lima Bean Casserole

1½ cups chopped broccoli
1½ cups green lima beans (baby limas preferred)
½ cup chopped water chestnuts
½ cup minced onion
1 (12-oz.) can cream of chicken or mushroom soup
1 cup sour cream
¼ cup diced sweet red bell peppers
buttered crushed corn flakes

Cook lima beans and broccoli in lightly salted water.
If using frozen vegetables, allow them to thaw completely.
Lightly butter baking dish.
Mix all ingredients together and pour into baking dish.
Top with crushed buttered corn flakes.
Bake in 350° oven 45 minutes.
Serves 6

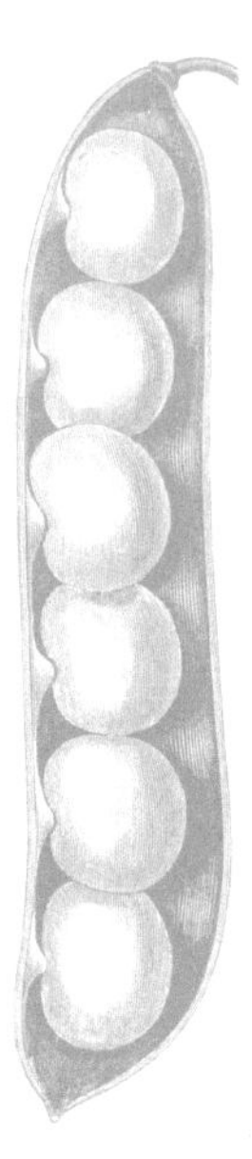

Macaroni and Cheese

1 cup small elbow macaroni
1 cup shredded Cheddar cheese
2 large eggs beaten
2½ cups milk
1 tablespoon grated onion
¼ teaspoon salt
dash of Tobasco sauce
½ cup shredded cheese
½ cup buttered bread crumbs

Cook macaroni according to directions on box
in lightly salted water. When done, rinse and drain as directed.
Set aside. Beat eggs, add milk, salt and Tabasco sauce.
Butter a baking dish.
Layer bottom with macaroni and cover with cheese.
Make another layer of macaroni and then cheese.
Pour milk, eggs, etc. over the casserole.
Top with the ½ cup cheese and ½ cup crumbs
which have been mixed together.
Bake in 375° oven until topping is lightly browned,
about 20 minutes.
Serves 6.
Buttered green peas are a nice accompaniment.

Potato Peas Casserole

3 cups fresh or frozen peas
1 cup pared and finely diced potatoes
6 slices bacon or ¾ cup seasoned sausage
2 tablespoons bacon or sausage drippings
2 tablespoons flour
1 cup milk
⅓ cup Parmesan mixed with buttered bread crumbs or crushed potato chips

Thaw peas, if they are frozen.
Mix together the vegetables and the bacon or sausage.
Using 2 tablespoons of the drippings in pan in which the meat has been sautéed, mix flour in drippings and blend until smooth.
Add milk slowly, stir and add a tablespoon or more if sauce seems too thick.
Combine meat, vegetables and sauce until well mixed.
Pour into greased 1½ or 2 quart casserole.
Mix Parmesan cheese with buttered bread crumbs or chips and cover top of casserole generously.
Bake in 325-350° oven about 50 minutes.
Serves 5-6

Red Kidney Bean Casserole

¾ cup chicken or ham broth
1 cup steamed rice
2 cups kidney beans
1½ cups sliced frankfurters or diced cooked ham
½ one small clove of garlic (minced)
¼ cup diced green pepper
¼ cup minced onion
1 egg beaten
dash Tabasco sauce
buttered bread or cracker crumbs

Butter 1½ quart casserole dish.
Mix together first seven ingredients.
Beat egg well, add Tabasco sauce to it and
mix it thoroughly with other ingredients.
Pour into baking dish. Top with crumbs.
Bake at 375° thirty minutes.
Reduce heat to 350° and bake another 15 minutes
or until crumbs are lightly browned.
Serves 6

Tasty Corn Bake

2 tablespoons butter or margarine
1 (8-oz.) package cream cheese
1 (16-oz.) bag frozen whole kernal corn thawed or 4 cups fresh sweet corn right off the cob
¼ cup minced sweet red pepper
⅓ cup milk (heated)
½ teaspoon salt
½ teaspoon garlic powder
dash Tabasco sauce

Melt butter, add cream cheese, blend well,
add hot milk and blend well.
Mix corn and red pepper and put in buttered baking dish.
Add seasonings to cream cheese mix and hot milk.
Stir and pour over corn and red peppers in baking dish.
Mix all together.
Bake in 350° oven about 25 minutes
or until it is nice and bubbly.
Serves 4-6

Potatoes, Peas and Ham Casserole

2 cups cooked and diced potatoes
1 cup green peas
1 ½ cups cooked and diced ham
½ cup minced onion
¼ cup minced sweet red pepper
dash of Tabasco sauce
2 tablespoons butter
2 tablespoons flour
1 ½ cups milk

Put first five ingredients in large bowl.
Melt butter in saucepan.
Add flour and stir until blended with butter.
Slowly add milk and stir until bubbly.
Stir in Tabasco sauce and a bit of salt if potato water was not salted.
Mix all together well and pour into buttered baking dish.
Bake in 350° oven 45-50 minutes.
Serves 6

Baked Beans and Ground Beef

1 pound ground beef
½ cup minced onion
¾ cup brown sugar
½ cup tomato ketchup
1 level tablespoon prepared mustard
1 teaspoon Worcestershire sauce
1 (28-oz.) can baked beans

Sauté ground beef in one tablespoon butter until lightly browned,
add onion and cook a minute or so.
Sprinkle lightly with salt and pepper if desired.
Mix beans with rest of ingredients and
pour into pan you wish to cook it in.
Add beef and onion to pan or pot. Simmer 30-35 minutes.
If dish seems too thick, add half cup or so of beef
or ham broth, or water.
Stir and simmer a few more minutes.
This dish is good served with or over mashed potatoes
or steamed rice.
Serves 6

Ham and Noodle Bake

1 ½ cups fine noodles
1 cup finely diced or ground cooked ham
½ cup shredded Cheddar cheese
⅓ cup finely diced green pepper
½ cup finely chopped celery
1 tablespoon minced onion
1 ½ cups milk
2 eggs
¾ cup buttered bread or cracker crumbs

Cook noodles according to package directions.
Rinse in cold water and drain.
Mix noodles together with the next five ingredients.
Beat eggs, add milk, pour over noodles, ham, etc.
Mix all together well and put in buttered baking dish.
Top with buttered crumbs.
Bake in 350° oven about 45 minutes.
Serves 6

Spinach Bacon Casserole

2 (10-oz.) packages frozen chopped spinach
8 slices sautéed and crumbled bacon
6 eggs
4 cups cottage cheese
2½ cups shredded sharp Cheddar cheese
2 tablespoons minced onion
1½ teaspoons salt
6 tablespoons flour
1 cup buttered bread crumbs

Thaw spinach completely. Do not drain.
Place spinach in large pan or bowl.
Add bacon, cottage cheese, Cheddar cheese and onion.
Beat together eggs, flour and salt. Pour over spinach.
Mix all together well. Pour into 9 x 13 x 3 inch casserole.
Cover top with buttered bread crumbs.
Bake in 350° oven 45 minutes or until contents have set
or baked through well.
Serves 12

(see photo page 35)

Yummy Hominy Cheese-Bacon

2 cups canned hominy
½ cup minced onion
½ cup minced sweet green pepper
¾ cup shredded Cheddar cheese
4 slices bacon sautéed and crumbled
2 tablespoons butter
1 ½ tablespoons flour
1 cup hot milk
½ teaspoon salt and dash of pepper if desired.

Mix hominy, onion, green pepper, bacon and shredded cheese in large bowl. In skillet melt butter, add flour and blend with butter. Slowly add the cup of milk to the flour mix and continue to stir the sauce until nicely blended. Mix sauce with other ingredients and pour into greased baking dish. Bake in 350° to 375° oven about 25 minutes. Check to see it doesn't become too brown.

Serves 6

Blackeye Pea Casserole

3 cups blackeye peas (fresh cooked or canned with their broth)
1 cup pared and finely diced potatoes
6 slices bacon sautéed and crumbled
¼ cup minced celery
¼ cup minced onion
⅔ cup buttered bread crumbs or coarsely crumbled potato chips
1 tablespoon bacon drippings or butter
1 tablespoon flour
1 cup milk

Butter bottom of 1½ or 2 quart casserole.
In skillet, add flour to drippings or butter, stir and blend well, gradually add milk and stir until it thickens.
Mix all ingredients together except the bread crumbs or potato chips.
Pour peas, etc. into casserole dish.
Top with crumbs or chips.
Bake in 325-350° oven until crumbs are lightly browned and crisp, about 50-55 minutes.
Serves 4-6

Baked Kidney Beans and Rice

3 cups cooked kidney beans and their juices
1½ cups cooked rice
1/4 cup pimento bits
1½ cups sautéed and crumbled bacon
1/2 cup minced onion (sautéed in bacon drippings)
1 cup crushed potato chips or shredded and buttered bread crumbs

Place one half the rice in a buttered casserole,
sprinkle with half of the pimento peppers.
Cover with one half of the crumbled bacon.
Cover bacon with one half of the kidney beans.
Repeat process until all ingredients have been added to casserole.
Top casserole with buttered bread crumbs
or crushed potato chips.
Bake in 325° oven 35-45 minutes.
Serves 6

Vegetarian Jambolaya

2 cups cooked rice
¾ pound small mushrooms (sliced)
1 medium size green pepper (finely chopped)
1 scant cup minced onion
1 cup finely chopped celery
1 small can pimento peppers (minced)
1¼ cups cooked and chopped tomatoes
1 stick butter
1 teaspoon sugar
salt to taste
shredded and buttered bread crumbs (optional)

Sauté washed mushrooms lightly in butter.
Add onion and sauté briefly. Add sugar to tomatoes.
Mix rice and all other ingredients together.
Pour well mixed ingredients into buttered casserole.
Top with buttered bread crumbs if desired or garnish with a few reserved mushrooms or green peppers or pimento peppers.

This recipe can serve as a base for other jambolaya dishes.
It is very good with sautéed pork sausage or bacon.

Bake dish in a 300° oven about one hour.
Serves 6-8

(see photo page 36)

Old-Fashioned Escalloped Tomatoes

3 cups ripe tomatoes, fresh skinned or stewed
½ cup minced green pepper
½ tablespoon finely minced or grated onion
2 teaspoons white or brown sugar
1 teaspoon salt or to taste
¼ teaspoon pepper or to taste
3-4 tablespoons melted butter
2 cups soft shredded and buttered bread crumbs

Butter bottom of 1½ quart casserole.
Place layer of bread crumbs in bottom of casserole.
Mix together tomato, green pepper, onion and sugar.
Add salt and pepper to taste.
Spoon ½ tomato mixture over bread crumbs.
Cover tomatoes with layer of crumbs.
Add remaining tomato mix and top generously
with remaining crumbs.
Bake uncovered in 375 degree oven until tomatoes are bubbly
and crumb topping is nicely browned.
Serves 6

Years ago we drizzled the melted butter over the tomato mix instead of buttering the crumbs. The top layer of crumbs may also be mixed with ½ cup shredded Cheddar cheese or ¼ cup Parmesan cheese if you like.

Browned Butter Macaroni and Tomatoes

3 cups cooked macaroni
1 stick butter or margarine
4 frankfurters (sliced)
1½ cups canned tomatoes
1½ tablespoons brown sugar
⅓ cup minced green pepper
dash Tabasco sauce
1 cup buttered Ritz cracker crumbs
½ cup shredded Cheddar cheese or grated Parmesan cheese

Cook macaroni according to package directions.
Brown butter (stir so as not to burn).
Sauté frankfurters briefly in brown butter. Add green pepper.
Toss butter, frankfurters, and green pepper with cooked and well-drained macaroni.
Chop tomatoes into small chunks, add brown sugar and Tabasco sauce. Mix well.
Add tomatoes, etc. to macaroni, frankfurters.
Add a bit more tomato juice if necessary.
Pour into casserole.
Mix buttered Ritz crumbs and cheese of your choice and sprinkle evenly on top of casserole.
Bake in 350° oven for 35-40 minutes and topping is lightly browned.
Creamed green peas or spinach is good served with it.
Casserole serves 6.

Great Northern Bean Casserole

4 cups cooked Great Northern Beans or 2(15½ oz.) cans
½ cup finely minced green spring onions
1 cup cooked, finely diced potatoes
8 slices sautéed bacon or 1 cup cooked, diced ham
1 tablespoon minced pimento pepper
1½ cups ham broth
2 tablespoons flour
2 cups coarsely shredded and buttered bread crumbs
½ cup grated Parmesan cheese

Sauté bacon and crumble it. Pour off most of the drippings.
Stir onions in remaining drippings. In large bowl, mix together
beans and bacon or ham and onions.
Mix together ham broth and flour until well blended.
Mix together beans, potatoes, bacon and onions
(or ham and onions) and pimento pepper .
Stir and blend in ham broth and flour.
Pour all into lightly buttered casserole.
Mix together buttered crumbs and Parmesan cheese
and spread over bean casserole.
Bake in 325-350° oven about 45 minutes or the crumbs etc.
are crisp and lightly browned.
A nice green salad on the side goes very nicely with it.
About 8 servings

Mashed Potatoes and Pork Sausage

2 pounds country-style pork sausage
3-4 potatoes (3 cups cubed)
1½ tablespoons butter
½ cup half and half milk
Salt and pepper to taste
1 beaten egg
½ cup shredded Cheddar or American cheese

Sauté sausage lightly. Do not brown. Mash potatoes in mixer.
Add butter, half and half, salt and pepper.
Add more half and half and butter if needed.
Beat potatoes until they are nice and fluffy.
Place half of the sautéed sausage in lightly buttered casserole.
Cover sausage with half of the mashed potatoes.
Spread remaining sausage over mashed potatoes.
Cover that sausage with the remaining potatoes.
Smooth over the mashed potatoes.
Beat the egg, blend in the shredded cheese.
Pour mixture over top of the mashed potatoes.
Bake in moderate oven 350 degrees about 30 minutes
and egg and cheese mix is nicely set.
This is an excellent way to use leftover mashed potatoes
which would already have been seasoned with
butter, half and half, etc.
A fresh green salad goes well with this dish.
Serves 6

Chicken Corn Pea Casserole

2 cups kernel or crushed corn
1 cup cooked, diced chicken
1 cup green peas
1 cup chicken broth or milk
1 tablespoon melted butter
1 tablespoon flour
2 teaspoons sugar (optional)
Salt and pepper to taste
Coarsely shredded buttered bread crumbs

Mix corn, chicken and peas together.
Melt butter in saucepan over medium heat.
Add flour, blend well. Slowly add broth or milk, stirring constantly.
Cook until mixture thickens.
Season with salt, pepper, and add sugar if desired.
Mix sauce with chicken, etc. Turn into buttered casserole.
Top with bread crumbs. Bake in 350-degree oven about 35 minutes
or until all ingredients are done and topping is
crispy and lightly browned.
Serves 6

Browned Butter Macaroni

3 cups cooked elbow macaroni
1 stick butter
2 cups hot milk
½ cup minced red bell pepper or pimento pepper
½ to ⅔ cup grated Parmesan cheese

Brown butter in saucepan, being careful not to burn.
Toss macaroni that has been cooked in lightly salted water.
Add a light sprinkle of pepper if desired.
Pour hot milk over macaroni and pour into lightly buttered casserole.
Cover generously with Parmesan cheese.
Dot casserole with bits of minced pepper.
Bake in 325° oven about 35 minutes.
Serves 4-6

Holiday Brunch Casserole

1¼ pounds loose country sausage, sautéed
1¼ cups coarsely grated Cheddar cheese
4 slices white bread, crumbled
7 eggs, beaten
2 cups milk
½ teaspoon dry mustard
1 tablespoon melted butter
½ cup grated Parmesan cheese

Toss bread crumbs with butter and Parmesan cheese.
Line a 9 x 13 x 3" buttered casserole with ⅔ of
the buttered crumbs/cheese mix.
Blend together the beaten eggs, milk, and dry mustard.
Mix together one cup of the Cheddar cheese with the sautéed
sausage. Blend together the sausage/cheese mix with milk and eggs.
Mix all together well and pour into crumb lined casserole.
Combine the remaining ¼ cup Cheddar cheese
with the bread and Parmesan cheese mix.
Cover the filled casserole with the mixture.
Bake in a 350° oven about 35 minutes or
until topping is crisp and lightly browned.
The casserole may also be made a day ahead, refrigerated
and baked the following day.
Great for holidays and busy weekends.
Serves 6-8 generously

Egg and Sausage Casserole

2½ cups shredded and buttered bread crumbs, day or so old bread
1 pound seasoned country sausage
1 cup shredded sharp Cheddar cheese
⅓ cup finely minced onion
½ cup shredded Swiss cheese
8 eggs, beaten
2 cups milk
½ tablespoon minced pimento pepper
1 tablespoon flour
salt and pepper to taste, very little if sausage is highly seasoned.

Sauté sausage in skillet until lightly browned.
Remove from heat and drain well, set aside.
Use about 2 tablespoons of the sausage drippings
to sauté onion and pimento pepper lightly.
Beat eggs and mix together with milk, cheeses, and flour.
Add seasonings and sausage, onion and pimento pepper.
Pour all into buttered casserole. Top with buttered crumbs.
Add a little Parmesan cheese to crumbs if desired.
You may substitute bacon for the sausage if desired.
Bacon, too, would need to be sautéed.
Bake at 325-350° about 35 minutes or until the eggs are set
and the crumbs are lightly browned.
Serves 6-8

Egg and Sausage Medley

1 pound bulk pork sausage
2 cups shredded bread crumbs (day or two-day old bread)
6 eggs, slightly beaten
2 cups milk
1 teaspoon salt (if sausage has not been salted)
½ teaspoon dry mustard
½ cup minced onion
1 cup cream of mushroom soup or sliced, fresh mushrooms
Buttered crumbs and Parmesan cheese topping

Sauté sausage until lightly browned but not overly cooked.
Drain off excess fat, sauté onions briefly.
Mix beaten eggs, milk, salt, mustard, bread crumbs, sautéed onion and mushroom soup or mushrooms. Mix all together well.
Pour into buttered casserole.
Cover top lightly with bread crumbs and sprinkle of Parmesan cheese.
Refrigerate overnight.
This recipe is wonderful for a holiday breakfast or brunch.
Bake in 350-degree oven about 40 minutes and top is lightly browned and crisp.
Serves 5-6

(see photo page 97)

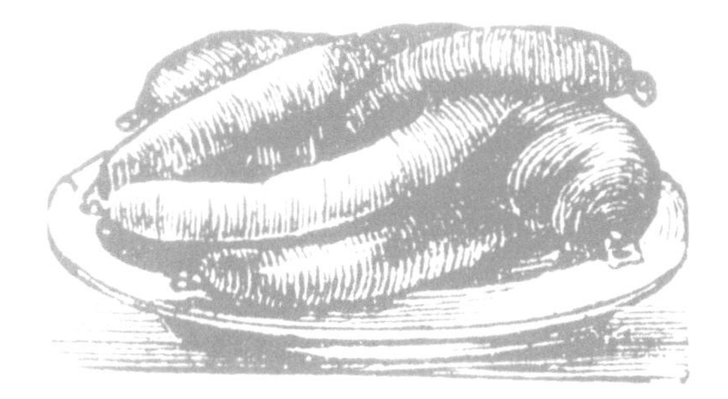

If we had never experienced a chilling rain,
falling for hours,
we would never fully appreciate the glorious sunshine
that follows the showers.

Fish & Shellfish

Shrimp Soufflé

½ stick butter or margarine
¼ cup flour
1 ½ cups milk
3 eggs separated
1 ½ cups freshly cooked or frozen shrimp
¼ teaspoon salt
dash or two Tabasco sauce
¼ cup finely minced celery
¼ cup finely minced green Bell pepper

If frozen, thaw shrimp, if precooked and deveined, remove tail.
If fresh, wash, boil in salt water until they turn pink,
about 10-15 minutes. Rinse in cold water.
Remove shells and deveine shrimp.
If shrimp are large, cut into 2-3 pieces. Rinse again and set aside.
Prepare sauce. Melt butter in sauce pan.
Blend in flour but do not allow to brown.
Slowly add milk, stir until sauce begins to thicken.
Add and beat in egg yolk a bit at a time. Blend well.
Add shrimp and seasonings. Add minced celery and peppers.
Beat egg whites until they peak well, but are not dry.
Fold egg whites into the cooled sauce and shrimp mixture.
Pour all into buttered casserole.
Bake in 350° oven 45-50 minutes until soufflé is set and firm.
Serve immediately.
Serves 4-6

Quick Crab Newburg

1 pound crabmeat, backfin or blend
1 (20 ounce) can cream of mushroom soup
1½ cups milk
¼ cup minced green or Pimento pepper
¼ cup dry sherry or 2 tablespoons lemon juice
dash Tabasco sauce

Pick over crab meat to remove shell or cartilage.
Flake crabmeat well.
In a sauce pan combine mushroom soup and milk.
Simmer and stir until well blended. Add green or Pimento pepper.
Add sherry or lemon juice. Adjust seasoning to taste. Mix well.
Fold in crabmeat, heat to boiling point but do not boil.
Serve immediately. Very good served over buttered triangles
of toast, mashed potatoes or steamed rice.
Serves 5-6

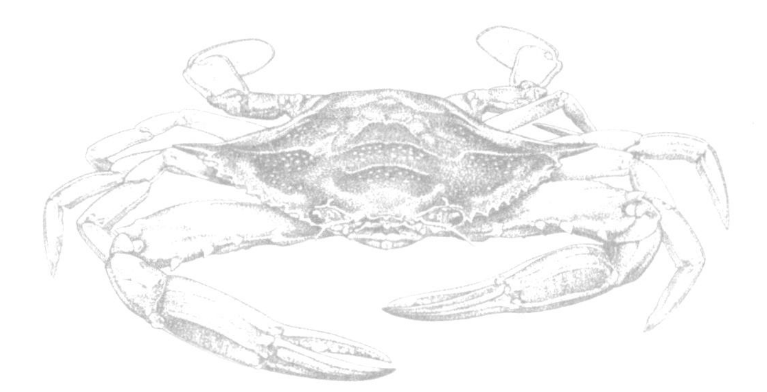

Crab Cakes

1 pound, special or backfin crabmeat
1 tablespoon butter
¼ cup finely minced onion
¼ cup finely minced green pepper
½ cup cracker meal or fine dry bread crumbs
2 beaten eggs
½ teaspoon Old Bay seasoning
3 tablespoons mayonnaise
extra fine bread crumbs for coating cakes

Check crabmeat for bits of shell or cartilage. Sauté onion in butter.
Mix together crabmeat, onion, green pepper, beaten egg
and Old Bay until blended well.
Add cracker meal or bread crumbs and mayonnaise.
Mix all together well. Divide mixture into 6-8 even portions.
Form each portion into ½ inch thick cakes.
Coat cakes with crumbs and pat into firm cakes.
Fry cakes in melted butter or cooking oil.
Brown on one side, turn cakes carefully and brown other side.
Serve hot with small dish of cocktail sauce
or mustard on the side.
Yields 6-8 cakes.

Creamed Crab

2 tablespoons butter
2 tablespoons flour
1¼ cups milk
½ tablespoon Worcestershire Sauce or lemon juice
¼ cup finely minced green pepper or pimento pepper
1 cup flaked crab meat
Dash Tabasco Sauce
¼ teaspoon thyme (optional)
Small bits of fresh parsley (optional)

Melt butter in saucepan. Add flour and stir until well blended.
Add milk slowly, stirring continuously until a smooth sauce is formed.
Add Worcestershire Sauce or lemon juice.
Add minced green pepper or pimento bits. Stir well.
Add Tabasco Sauce and crab meat. Add a bit of salt if needed.
Add the thyme if you like. Mix all together well.
The bits of parsley may be added at this time.
If the creamed crab meat seems to be too thick, blend in
a bit more milk, stirring as you add the milk until it becomes
the proper consistency to spoon over buttered toast,
mashed potatoes, or steamed rice.
This recipe may also be used to make creamed shrimp.
Substitute shrimp for the crab meat.
If shrimp are large, each shrimp should be cut
into two or three pieces.
Serves 4

Quick and Easy Baked Fish

1½ pounds fish fillets (halibut, haddock, swordfish)
½ cup slivered almonds
½ cup melted butter
2 tablespoons lemon juice
Salt and pepper
Paprika and snipped parsley

Lightly butter or grease a shallow baking dish.
Place fillets singly in baking dish.
Mix lemon juice and melted butter and drizzle over each fillet.
Sprinkle almonds and lightly salt and pepper fillets.
Cover baking dish with foil and bake at
350° about 12-15 minutes.
Remove foil and bake another 12-15 minutes or until
fish flakes easily when tested with fork.
Sprinkle fillets lightly with paprika and garnish
with snipped parsley.
Serves 4

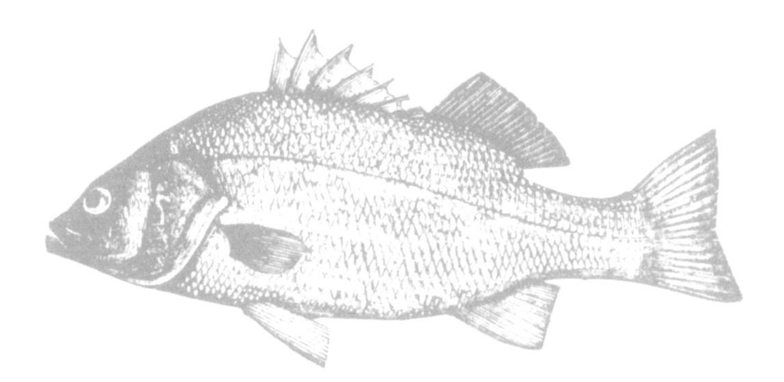

Creamed Fish

2 tablespoons butter
2 tablespoons flour
1 cup milk or half and half
1 cup flaked crab meat, shrimp or flaked fish
¼ teaspoon salt
¼ cup minced pimento or green pepper
2 teaspoons prepared mustard (optional)

Melt butter in saucepan. Add flour and stir until blended.
Add milk or half and half gradually and stir continuously
and bring to a low boil. Add salt, minced pimento or green pepper.
Cook a minute or so until sauce is well blended.
Add fish or seafood and a few bits of snipped parsley.
If sauce seems too thick, add a bit more milk and stir well.
This makes a nice quick luncheon dish when served
over toast or hot biscuits.
May be made with leftover fish or other seafood.
Serves 4

Baked Fish Fillets

2 pounds fresh fish fillets (halibut, haddock, tilapia)
Liquid Smoke or Worcestershire Sauce
Garlic or garlic salt
Buttered bread crumbs
Parmesan cheese (about ½ cup)

Mix bread crumbs with Parmesan cheese.
Rub fillets with halved clove of garlic
or sprinkle lightly with garlic salt.
Brush fillets with Liquid Smoke or Worcestershire Sauce.
Pat fillets generously with buttered bread crumbs
and place fillets singly in buttered baking dish or pan.
Bake in 350° oven about 15 minutes or until fillets are done
and flake when tested with a fork.
Raise oven temperature a bit and place fish on top rack
in oven for just a minute or two, if the crumbs need to be
made a bit more crisp.
Thin slices of lemon are a nice garnish for the serving platter.
Serves 6

Salmon Potato Cakes

2 cups cold mashed potatoes
1 cup flaked salmon, canned or leftover fillet
1 egg beaten
1 teaspoon Worcestershire Sauce or 2 teaspoons lemon juice or dry sherry
Dash hot sauce
Crushed and buttered corn flakes or buttered bread crumbs

Check salmon to remove bones.
Mix flaked salmon, mashed potatoes, beaten egg, and either Worcestershire Sauce, lemon juice, or dry sherry and hot sauce.
Pat into ½" thick round cakes.
Cover with either corn flakes or bread crumbs.
Pat into firm cakes. Fry in melted butter or bacon drippings.
A small container of honey mustard or tomato ketchup goes well with the hot fried cakes.
Yield 6-7 cakes

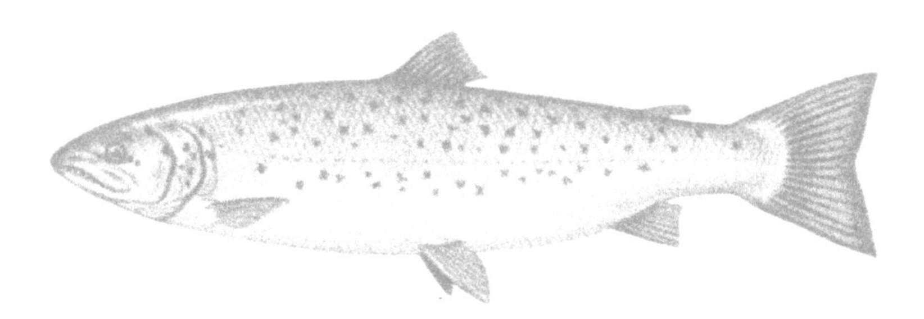

Shrimp Newburg

2½ cups cleaned, shelled, deveined, and cooked shrimp
2 tablespoons butter
2 tablespoons flour
1 cup half and half
2½ tablespoons tomato ketchup
½ tablespoon Worcestershire Sauce
Salt to taste
Dash Tabasco sauce
2 tablespoons dry sherry (optional)

Remove shrimp tails if still on.
If shrimp are large, cut into 2 to 3 pieces. Melt butter in saucepan.
Stir in flour and blend well. Slowly add half and half.
Stir and blend well. When sauce is nice and smooth, add seasonings,
the tomato ketchup, Worcestershire Sauce and salt to taste.
Add Tabasco sauce. If sauce seems too thick,
add a bit more half and half. Add shrimp.
Mix well and keep hot until serving time.
Add sherry just before serving.
A sprinkle of snipped parsley may be added.
The Newburg is good served over steamed rice,
buttered noodles, or cooked sea shells.
Serves 4

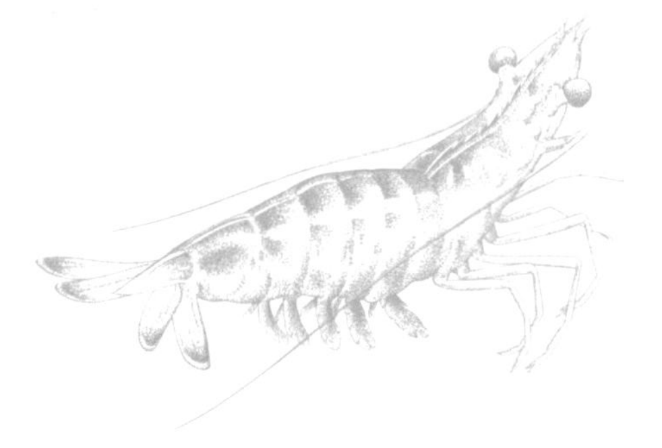

Easy Broiled Salmon

4 (6-ounce) salmon fillets
Olive or Wesson oil
Garlic salt and garlic pepper
¼ cup dry sherry
4 green spring onions
1 teaspoon dill weed
2 teaspoons lemon juice
1 stick butter

Brush fillets with olive or Wesson oil on both sides.
Sprinkle lightly with garlic salt and garlic pepper
on both sides of fillets.
Place fillets in pan and broil in hot oven about 10 minutes,
being careful not to burn fillets.
When fillets will flake, remove from oven
and place on serving platter.
Set where it may be kept warm until oven cools.
When oven cools down, return platter with fillets to keep hot.
Pour sherry into saucepan. Add finely sliced green onions.
Bring to boil. Add dill weed and lemon juice.
Lower heat and simmer until liquid has cooked down
to several tablespoonfuls.
Add butter and stir carefully allowing butter
to melt and blend completely.
Spoon hot sauce over fillets and serve immediately.
Serves 4

Easy Baked Oysters

1 pint oysters
1 cup crumbled white bread crumbs
4 tablespoons butter or margarine
2 tablespoons grated Parmesan cheese
Light sprinkle garlic salt
5 strips bacon cut in ½" pieces

Drain oysters well. Melt butter in saucepan.
Mix bread crumbs, garlic salt, and Parmesan cheese.
Turn into melted butter in saucepan. Stir and lightly brown.
Pour drained oysters into a buttered baking dish.
Cover oysters with browned crumb mix.
Arrange bacon pieces evenly over crumb mix.
Place into 450 degree oven and bake 20-25 minutes
and bacon is crisp and browned.
Serves 4

Oyster Pie

1 pint oysters
¼ cup finely minced onion
2 tablespoons butter
2 tablespoons flour
1½ cups milk
½ teaspoon salt or celery salt to taste
1 rich pie pastry for topping

Drain oysters well. Sauté minced onion in melted butter.
Add flour and blend well. Slowly add milk.
Stir and blend until sauce is smooth. Add salt or celery salt to taste.
Add drained oysters to sauce and pour into buttered pie pan.
Top with rich pie pastry. Crimp edges.
Make several slashes in topping.
Bake in 450 degree oven for 20 minutes or
until crust is golden brown.
Serves 4-6

Shrimp and Sea Shells

1 cup finely minced onion
1 cup finely diced celery
4 tablespoons melted butter or bacon drippings
2 tablespoons flour
1 cup water
1½ cups cooked crushed or finely chopped tomatoes
1 tablespoon lemon juice
2 teaspoons sugar
1 cup sliced mushrooms and juice
Salt and pepper to taste
One dash of Tabasco
1 (24-ounce) package frozen shrimp
1 (8-ounce) package small sea shells

Thaw shrimp, remove tails, and if large, cut in halves.
Sauté onion and celery in melted butter or bacon drippings.
When celery and onions are about half done,
add flour and cup of water. Stir until well blended.
Blend in lemon juice, tomatoes, sugar, salt and pepper, Tabasco,
mushrooms and juice. Adjust seasonings to taste.
Stir in shrimp that has been thawed and tails removed.
Reduce heat and simmer until all ingredients are well seasoned.
Cook sea shells according to package directions.
When done, rinse and drain well. Toss with melted butter if desired.
Serve hot shrimp and sauce in one bowl and the sea shells
in another or place sea shells in one large bowl
and cover with the shrimp sauce.
Serves 6-8 generously.

Meat & Poultry

Tasty Sausage Cakes

1 pound seasoned "country" pork sausage
¼ cup crushed and drained pineapple
⅓ cup dry bread crumbs
2 tablespoons flour
1 tablespoon light brown sugar
1 beaten egg

Combine sausage, pineapple, bread crumbs,
brown sugar and beaten egg.
Mix well and form into small flat sausage cakes.
Pat generously with flour. Place in lightly greased skillet.
Brown quickly on both sides but don't allow them to burn.
Cut heat to very low. Cover cakes with lid and allow them
to slowly cook until done through. Serve while hot.
Applesauce, sprinkled with a bit of cinnamon and sugar,
well blended, is a nice side dish for the cakes
as well as warm corn bread.
Makes about 6 nice cakes, 8 if a bit smaller.

Yummy Chicken Patties

1 cup cooked, finely diced chicken
2 eggs slightly beaten
1 tablespoon half and half or cream
Fine plain bread crumbs
Light sprinkle crushed tarragon leaves
2 tablespoons butter
2 tablespoons flour
1 cup milk
Salt and pepper to taste
½ cup finely minced celery

Beat one egg, add half and half, and mix with chopped chicken.
Mix together dry bread crumbs and tarragon.
Pat damp patties with dry crumbs.
Dip patties into the other beaten egg.
Cover patties again with the dry crumbs and form them into small, flat, round cakes.
Makes five small well-breaded little cakes.
Fry in small amount of butter or fat and brown on both sides.
Do not have skillet too hot as they need to fry slowly to cook through well. Set patties aside in a warm place.
Make white sauce. Melt butter, add flour, stir and blend well.
Do not allow flour to brown.
Add milk slowly, add seasonings and minced celery.
Cook slowly until of right consistency to serve.
Add a bit more milk if necessary.
Place sauce over hot patties and serve.
A green vegetable is nice to serve with them.
Serves 3-4

Hamburger Steak Patties

1 ¼ pounds ground round steak
¾ cup shredded bread crumbs
1 egg
¾ teaspoon salt
½ teaspoon pepper
1 cup finely chopped tomatoes, freshly cooked or canned
1 tablespoon brown sugar
1 teaspoon lemon juice
⅛ teaspoon nutmeg (optional)
2 tablespoons melted butter or bacon drippings
¼ cup minced onion
1 tablespoon flour

Mix together ground beef, bread crumbs, egg, salt and pepper.
Pat into soft round, ½-inch thick cakes or patties.
Pat lightly with flour. Brown on both sides
in butter or bacon drippings.
Set aside in a place where they will remain hot.
Make a sauce of the essence left in the pan.
Sauté onions in the essence. Add flour.
Stir together tomatoes, brown sugar, lemon juice and nutmeg
which have been mixed together.
Simmer until all are well blended together.
Arrange hot meat patties on large serving platter.
Pour sauce over patties and serve.
A bowl of fluffy mashed potatoes are a nice accompaniment.
Serves 4-6

Roast Tenderloin of Beef

5-6 pound tenderloin of beef
salt and pepper (salt may be garlic salt)
flour
8-10 slices smoked bacon
snipped parsley

Remove tenderloin from refrigerator.
Remove any small bits of fat.
This is important as it will eliminate fatty spots when it is sliced.
Wipe fillet with paper towel. Turn fillet bottom side up.
Sprinkle it with plain or garlic salt and pepper.
Turn fillet top side up and repeat with salt and pepper.
Dust the fillet with flour. Place in roasting pan on wire rack.
Cover fillet with bacon slices. Secure slices with wooden picks.
Do not add water or cover pan. Roast in 300° oven
25 to 30 minutes per pound. Remove bacon.
Roast may be served immediately and cut
in ⅓ to ½ inch slices.

For parties, remove bacon.
When cold, place fillet in refrigerator over night.
Slice in very thin slices. Arrange on platters as you slice the fillet.
Decorate with parsley sprigs.
Horseradish on the side is good.

Country Fried Chicken

chicken pieces for frying, legs, thighs, breasts
flour
salt and pepper
butter, vegetable oil or lard

Wash and pat dry with paper towels each piece of chicken.
Mix flour, salt and pepper in large bowl or paper bag.
Cover each piece of chicken with the flour mix by rolling it in the bowl or shaking it in the bag.
Heat butter, vegetable oil or lard in a large heavy skillet.
When the fat is nice and hot, place the chicken pieces in the pan.
Do not overcrowd the chicken pieces. Fry the chicken on medium-high heat until one side is nicely browned. Turn chicken side and brown. Repeat with other pieces of chicken.
If you are frying only the pieces in the pan, pour off and reserve the fat. Add ½ cup or so of water to the pan.
Cover tightly and let chicken steam about 20 minutes or so.

If you wish to make gravy, remove chicken pieces from pan and place them where they will remain hot.
Replace several tablespoons of reserved fat into skillet and add 2-3 tablespoons of flour, stir and brown.
Add milk or half milk and half water, add salt and pepper to taste.
Blend all well and serve piping hot.

**When I fry a large number of chicken pieces, I place the fried pieces in a large roasting pan. Keep the pieces as hot as possible. When finished frying, I move the pan of chicken to the oven set at about 275°-300°, add a little water, cover with a tight lid or foil until the pieces are steaming hot.
Mashed potatoes and gravy are wonderful with the fried chicken.

(see photo page 98)

Beef Roast and Red Potatoes

6-7 pound rib eye roast of beef
bacon slices
salt and pepper
clove of garlic
6-8 small red potatoes

Pat roast dry with paper towel. Scrub and wash red potatoes.
Rub beef with cut garlic clove.
Sprinkle roast with salt and pepper on all sides.
Place on rack in roasting pan. Dust lightly with flour.
Cover roast with bacon slices.
Secure slices with wooden picks so the roast will remain well covered.
Do not cover or add water to roasting pan.
When about half of the roasting time has expired,
place potatoes around roast.
Baste them with pan drippings or butter several times
during remaining roasting time.
Roast beef in 300° oven 25 to 30 minutes per pound.
Check potatoes with sharp paring knife.
When meat and potatoes are done, remove from oven.
Remove bacon from roast.
Place beef on hot platter either whole or sliced.
Place potatoes around meat and sprinkle with bits
of fresh parsley if desired.
Serves 6-8.

(see photo page 163)

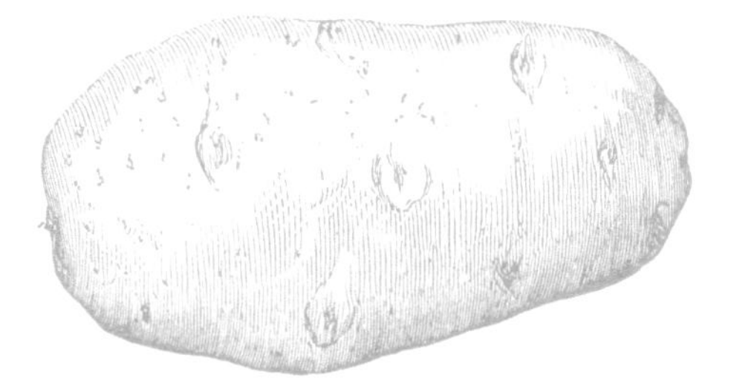

Hamburger Meat Loaf

1 ½ pounds good ground beef
2½ cups soft day-old bread crumbs
2 beaten eggs
¾ cup milk
½ cup Hunt's tomato sauce or crushed tomatoes
1 tablespoon sugar
½ cup finely minced onion
⅔ cup shredded Cheddar cheese
¼ teaspoon pepper
½ teaspoon garlic powder or juice (optional)
6-7 slices bacon
2-3 potatoes sliced in ⅛-inch slices

Mix beaten eggs, bread crumbs, eggs, milk, Hunt's tomato sauce or crushed tomatoes, sugar, onion, cheese, garlic with the ground beef. Add seasonings.
Pat into a nice firm oval-shaped roast.
Top with bacon slices to cover. Secure bacon with wooden picks.
Place baking pan in 325-degree oven.
Bake about 1½ to 2 hours or until bacon is slightly browned.
When roast is half done, layer potatoes around roast and bake with roast until potatoes and meat loaf are done.
Baste potatoes with pan drippings several times during baking time. Serve hot.
Serves 6

Old-Fashioned Stewed Chicken and Dumplings

6 pieces stewing chicken
½ cup minced onion
1 teaspoon salt
sprinkle of pepper

DUMPLINGS
1 cup sifted flour
2 teaspoons baking powder
⅛ teaspoon salt
2 tablespoons melted butter
1 egg
⅓ cup milk
1 tablespoon minced parsley

Wash and dry chicken pieces. Place in stew pot and cover with water. Add onion, salt and pepper. Bring to a boil, reduce heat and cook over medium heat until tender. Sift together flour, baking powder and salt. Beat egg, blend with melted butter, add milk and blend into flour mixture. Add snipped parsley. Add a bit more milk if necessary. The batter should be thick but not dry. Drop batter by scant tablespoons onto the simmering chicken pieces, not down into the boiling liquid. Cover quickly with tight lid. Cook over medium heat 12-15 minutes depending on the size of the dumplings.

When dumplings are done you may wish to make a gravy of the remaining broth. Arrange chicken and dumplings on a serving platter in a warm medium hot oven. Melt a tablespoon of butter in sauce pan, add 1 tablespoon flour and ½ cup milk. Stir and blend together until smooth. Pour sauce into chicken broth, stirring continually. If gravy is not quite thick enough, add a bit more milk and flour, blended together. A light sprinkle of garlic pepper over the chicken and dumplings will only make it better.

Serves 6

Easy Oven "Fried" Chicken

6-8 pieces frying chicken
1 stick melted butter
¾ cup fine bread crumbs
3 tablespoons Parmesan cheese
¾ teaspoon crushed oregano leaves
¾ teaspoon crushed basil leaves
¾ teaspoon garlic salt
¼ teaspoon plain or celery salt (optional)
Sprinkle garlic pepper

Mix together bread crumbs, Parmesan cheese, oregano leaves, basil leaves, garlic salt, celery salt, if desired, and garlic pepper. Place melted butter in one dish and crumb mix in another. Dip piece of chicken first in crumb mix, then in melted butter, and again in crumb mix. Place chicken piece, skin side down, in buttered shallow baking pan or casserole.
Repeat process with rest of chicken pieces.
Bake in 420-425 degree oven about 15 minutes.
Turn chicken pieces skin side up and bake about 30 minutes more or until chicken is nicely browned and well done.
Yield 6-8 pieces

Baked Pork Chops

6 pork chops
¼ cup melted butter
½ cup minced onion
3 cups shredded and well buttered bread crumbs
½ teaspoon celery salt, seasoning salt, or garlic salt
1 (10-ounce) can cream of mushroom soup

Sear pork chops on both sides in melted butter.
Placed seared pork chops in buttered baking disk.
Sauté onions in pan drippings. Add a bit more butter if necessary.
Mix buttered bread crumbs with sautéed onions and seasonings.
Spread mixture evenly over each chop.
Blend together mushroom soup and water.
Spoon evenly over each breaded chop.
Bake in 325 degree oven about 50-60 minutes.
Cover chops lightly for the first 25 or 30 minutes.
Remove covering for the remaining baking time.
Serves 6

Beef Burgundy

1½ pounds beef round steak
4 tablespoons flour, lightly seasoned with salt and pepper
4 tablespoons butter

3 tablespoons butter
⅔ cup finely minced onion
1½ cups small sliced fresh mushrooms or
1 (7⅓ ounce) jar of canned mushrooms
½ cup diagonally sliced carrots (optional)
3 tablespoons flour
2 cups canned beef broth or 4 bouillon cubes and two cups water
1 tablespoon Worcestershire Sauce
½-⅔ cup Burgundy wine to taste

Cut beef into ½" cubes. Dust them with the 4 tablespoons flour, salt and pepper that have been mixed together.
Melt 4 tablespoons butter in skillet and sauté the beef cubes on all sides until lightly browned. Set beef aside in warm place.
Melt the 3 tablespoons butter in another skillet or saucepan.
Sauté onions in butter and then the carrots until cooked through but not brown. Add the 3 tablespoons flour. Stir well.
Slowly add beef broth or bouillon cubes and water. Stir and blend.
Mix together sautéed beef and sautéed vegetables, etc.
Add a bit of beef broth or water if the mixture seems too thick.
If necessary, spoon all into a larger pan or pot.
Cover tightly with lid and place in a 300-325 degree oven.
Let it simmer slowly in oven. Stir occasionally.
Add a bit more liquid if it seems necessary.
At about 50 minutes cooking, test beef. If done, add Burgundy wine.
Stir well. Let it cook about 5-10 minutes longer.
Serve over steamed rice or even hot biscuits or mashed potatoes.
Serves 8

Egg & Sausage Medley

page 69

Country Fried Chicken
page 90

Shrimp Salad
page 110

Carrot Soufflé
page 125

Chicken Pot Pie with Cheese

1½ cups chicken broth
1½ cups peeled and diced potatoes
¾ cup carrots, sliced diagonally, or green peas
½ cup minced celery
½ cup minced onion
¼ cup flour
1½ cups milk
1 cup shredded American or sharp Cheddar cheese
3½ cups cooked and diced chicken
¼ teaspoon celery salt
Salt and pepper, season to taste

Prepare pastry for top of pie.

Pour chicken broth in stew pot.
Add all the vegetables and bring to boil.
Lower heat and simmer until vegetables are tender.
Blend together flour and milk and slowly stir into vegetable mixture.
Add cheese and stir until melted. Add celery salt and a bit of salt and pepper to taste, being careful not to over salt. Stir in chicken.
Mix well and pour into a 3-quart buttered casserole.
Top with prepared pastry, covering ingredients completely.
Make a few slashes in topping. Brush top with melted butter or milk.
Bake in 425 degree oven about 25-30 minutes or until crust is golden brown.
Serves 8-10

Pork Chops and Sauerkraut

6 thick pork chops
1 (20½-ounce) can or package sauerkraut
2½-3 cups well seasoned mashed potatoes
Sprinkle of light brown sugar and/or 1 teaspoon caraway or celery seed (optional)

Sear pork chops well on both sides in bacon drippings or butter.
Rinse sauerkraut in water, optional, and drain well.
Toss kraut with brown sugar and/or caraway or celery seed, if desired.
Butter bottom of casserole dish. Cover with one half of the kraut.
Place chops over kraut. Cover lightly with remaining kraut.
Cover and bake about one hour in a 325 degree oven.
Remove from oven. Place a large flower tip in pastry bag
and pipe warm mashed potatoes around base of chops and kraut.
Return to oven and bake about 10 minutes to reheat kraut, etc.
and lightly brown mashed potatoes.
If pastry bag is not available, with two tablespoons, simply
spread potatoes around base of chops.
If preferred, the mashed potatoes may be served in a side dish.
Serves 6

This recipe may also be used substituting a small roast of pork
instead of the chops.
In that case, add 30 minutes or so to baking time.

Roast Turkey Breast and Gravy

1 small turkey breast
Dressing
Cream gravy
Fresh sliced or canned mushrooms (optional)

Grease and roast small turkey breast.
Sprinkle lightly with salt about half way through roasting period.
Baste several times during roasting.
Cool and store in refrigerator until cold enough to slice well.
Slice into thin slices. Butter a 9 x 13" casserole.
Cover bottom with layer of your favorite dressing.
Cover with thin turkey slices. Sprinkle with mushroom slices
if you are using them. Cover generously with gravy.
Top with layer of your favorite dressing. Bake in moderate oven
about 35-40 minutes and dressing is lightly browned.
This recipe may also be made with leftover diced turkey
and gravy made from pan drippings.
May also be made with roast chicken and buttered,
shredded bread crumbs and creamed chicken gravy.
This dish may also be made in large quantities
to serve at larger gatherings.
A 9 x 13" casserole will serve 8-10 well.

A loaf of bread can feed a hungry body,

a word or act of kindness

can nourish a starving soul.

Salads & Dressings

Potato Salad Deluxe

4 cups cooked and diced potatoes
½ cup unpeeled diced cucumbers
2 tablespoons finely sliced or minced green onions
⅓ cup finely minced celery
1 cup finely minced green cabbage
1½ teaspoon salt
½ teaspoon ground pepper
4 hard-cooked eggs
1 cup sour cream
½ cup mayonnaise
¼ cup vinegar
½ cup sugar
1 teaspoon prepared mustard

Cook eggs in lightly salted water.
When done, peel and separate yolks and whites.
Combine prepared potatoes, onions, celery, cabbage, salt, pepper and chopped egg whites.
Reserve cucumbers until ready to serve as cucumbers have a tendency to weep if prepared too far ahead.
Mash egg yolks in mixer. Add sour cream, mayonnaise, vinegar, sugar and mustard. Toss all together and refrigerate.
Add diced cucumbers when ready to serve.
Serves 8-10

Best Macaroni Salad

8 ounces elbow macaroni
½ cup French dressing
¾ cup finely diced celery
½ cup minced sweet pickles
½-pound shredded Cheddar cheese
1½ cups finely cubed cooked ham
½ cup mayonnaise

Cook macaroni according to package directions.
Rinse cooked macaroni in cold water and drain.
Toss macaroni with French dressing.
Set aside to marinate while you are preparing other ingredients.
Mix together the celery, pickles, cheese, ham and mayonnaise.
Combine all ingredients together and toss well.
I sometimes add a tiny bit of sugar to mayonnaise,
but I like it just as well without.
Refrigerate until serving time.
Serves 6

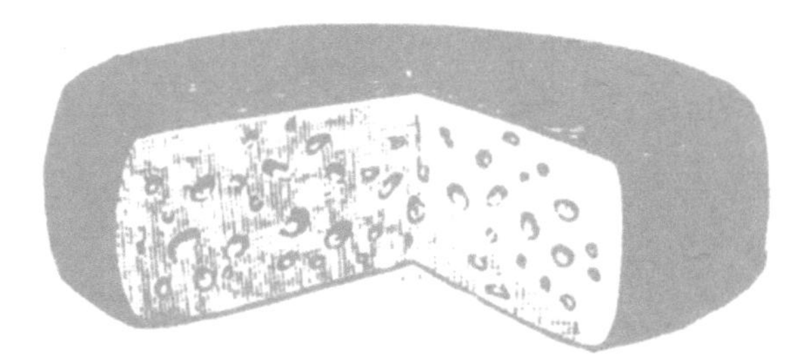

Sour Cream Potato Salad

4 cups potatoes (cooked in salted water, then diced)
½ cup unpeeled and finely diced cucumbers
¼ cup finely minced green spring onions
1 teaspoon salt
½ teaspoon ground pepper
½ cup minced celery
½ cup finely shredded green cabbage
3 hard-cooked eggs
1½ cups sour cream
½ cup mayonnaise
⅓ cup vinegar
⅓ cup sugar
1 teaspoon prepared mustard

Prepare all vegetables except the cucumbers
which should be added at serving time.
Toss vegetables with salt and pepper.
Separate cooked egg whites and yolks.
Dice whites and add to vegetables. In mixer, blend together sour cream, mayonnaise, vinegar, sugar, and mustard.
Blend in cooked egg yolks. Mix well. Adjust seasonings to taste.
Toss all together. Refrigerate.
*Add diced cucumbers when ready to serve.
Serves about 8

*Cucumbers have a tendency to weep if cut too far ahead.

Broccoli Salad

3 cups fresh broccoli, cut in small pieces
½ cup thinly sliced green spring onions
½ cup shredded American or sharp Cheddar cheese
½ cup crisp sautéed bacon pieces
½ cup mayonnaise
2 tablespoons sugar
1 tablespoon vinegar
Dash celery salt

Sauté bacon and drain it well.
Mix broccoli, onions and shredded cheese.
You may add ½ cup or so of finely chopped cauliflower if you like.
Add crisp bacon pieces. Make dressing.
Blend together mayonnaise, sugar, vinegar and celery salt.
Adjust sweet-sour dressing to your taste.
Toss dressing with refrigerated vegetables just before serving.
Serves 5-6

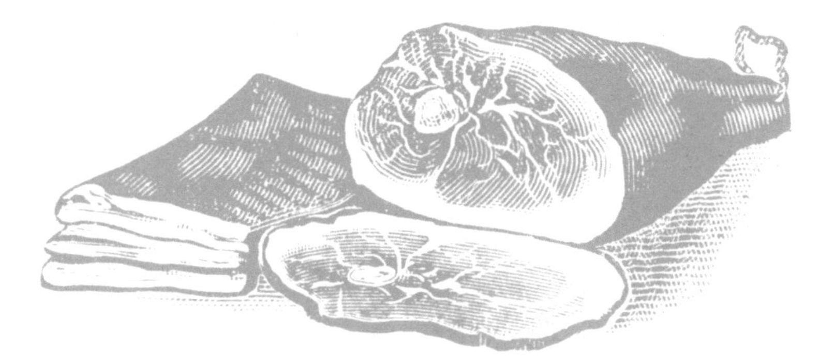

Shrimp Salad

1½ pounds shrimp (cooked and deveined)
3 tablespoons minced parsley
1½ cups chopped cauliflower, broccoli, or diced cucumber
1½ cups finely chopped celery
½ cup minced sweet pickle
2 cups small sea shells, cooked according to package directions
3 tablespoons tomato ketchup
¾ cup mayonnaise
1½ tablespoons lemon juice
1½ teaspoons finely minced onion
½ teaspoon salt or celery salt
Lettuce

If shrimp are large, cut into two or three pieces if desired.
Mix shrimp and cooked sea shells.
Add cauliflower, broccoli, or diced cucumber and pickle.
Make dressing with mayonnaise, tomato ketchup, lemon juice, minced onion (small spring onions are nice), salt or celery salt.
Toss together well. Chill well before serving.
Serve on individual plates on lettuce leaves or from a lettuce-lined salad bowl.
Serves 6

(see photo page 99)

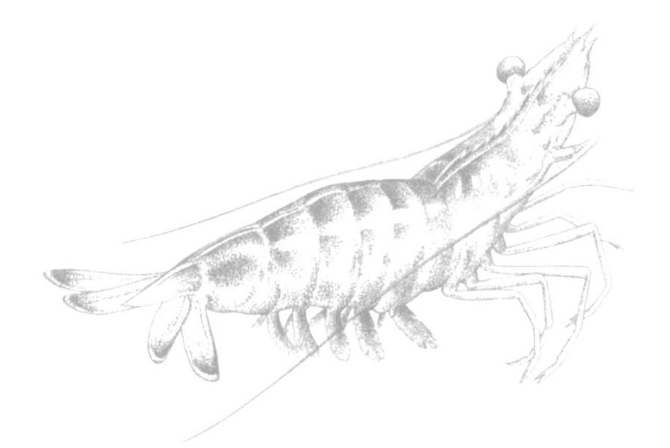

Ham and Potato Deluxe Salad

3 cups cooked and cubed potatoes
¾ cup mayonnaise
2 teaspoons prepared mustard
1 tablespoon vinegar
2 tablespoons sugar
½ teaspoon salt
2 cups cubed fully cooked ham
4 hard-cooked eggs (dice 3 and reserve 1 for garnish)
¾ cup diced unpeeled cucumber or zucchini
½ cup small red radishes, sliced
3 tablespoons minced celery
3 tablespoons red or green pepper (minced)
Parsley sprigs

Beat together mayonnaise, mustard, vinegar, sugar and salt.
Pour this dressing over potatoes. Let stand about 30 minutes.
Toss together all the rest of the ingredients.
Gently fold all together potatoes and dressing.
Add a bit more mayonnaise if salad is too dry.
Spoon into salad bowl which has been lightly lined
with lettuce leaves. Garnish salad with sliced egg and parsley sprigs.
Refrigerate until serving time.
Serves 8

Carrot Raisin Salad

1 cup seedless golden raisins
1½ cups finely shredded carrots
½ cup finely chopped celery
½ cup chopped English walnuts or sliced almonds
¼ teaspoon salt
1 teaspoon lemon juice
3 tablespoons sugar
Mayonnaise to moisten

Pour hot water over raisins and let set to plump up a bit.
Rinse and drain on paper towels.
Blend together well salt, lemon juice, and sugar.
Toss with raisins, carrots, celery, and nuts. Mix all together.
Fold in mayonnaise sufficient to moisten salad.
Refrigerate. Serve on lettuce leaves.
Serves 6

Creamy Ambrosia Salad

3 cups mandarin oranges, Clementines, or Naval oranges
2 sliced bananas (not overly ripe)
1 cup green grapes (halved)
½ cup golden seedless raisins or snipped dates
½ cup whipped topping
¼ cup mayonnaise
5-6 large marshmallows, snipped (optional)
½ cup freshly grated or flaked coconut

Drain peeled and diced mandarin oranges, Clementines or Naval oranges. Mix together the four fruits. Blend together whipped topping and mayonnaise. Add marshmallows, if desired. Fold all ingredients together. Spoon onto lettuce arranged on salad plates. Garnish each serving with coconut.
Serves 6-8

Hot "Greens" Salad

1 pound dandelion, turnip or other greens
6 slices bacon, cut in small pieces
¼ cup vinegar
1 teaspoon minced garlic or spring onions
2 tablespoons sour cream or half and half
1 egg or two egg yolks
¼ teaspoon salt

Discard coarse stems and discolored leaves of greens.
Wash through several changes of water. Break into small pieces.
Drain well and set aside. Sauté bacon until nicely browned.
Spoon off about ⅓ of the drippings. Sauté garlic or onions.
Remove bacon and garlic or onion from skillet.
Pour a tablespoon of water onto drippings.
Return bacon and garlic or onion to skillet.
Beat together egg with sour cream or half and half,
the vinegar and salt. Pour over bacon, etc. Bring to boil.
Pour over greens that have been set aside
and toss until greens are wilted.
My mother-in-law in the early 1930s returned the greens
to the sauce in the skillet and heated them a bit more.
This sauce may be used with mustard greens,
collard greens, and watercress.
The greens are delicious served with mashed or
pan-fried potatoes or corn bread.
Serves 4-6

Vegetable Dishes

Potatoes Divine

4 cups potatoes, diced small and cooked briefly in lightly salted water
1 (16-oz.) can cream of chicken soup
2 cups sour cream
8 slices bacon, sautéed and cut into fine pieces
1 small to medium size onion, minced and sautéed in bacon drippings
1 pound shredded Cheddar cheese
½ stick melted butter
salt and pepper to taste
1½ cups crushed potato chips or crushed and buttered Ritz crackers

Mix together potatoes (which have been drained), chicken soup, sour cream, shredded cheese, onion, bacon, salt and pepper, if needed. Mix well.
Pour all into 9 x 13 x 2 inch casserole.
Drizzle with melted butter and cover top with potato chips or Ritz cracker crumbs.
Bake in 350° oven about one hour.
Serves 10-12

Lima Beans Deluxe

3½ cups fresh green lima beans
3 tablespoons melted butter
1 teaspoon sugar
1⅓ cups half and half cream (heated)
2 egg yolks (beaten)
½ tablespoon flour
¼ teaspoon salt
½ cup snipped parsley

Cook lima beans in lightly salted water.
Mix in a small bowl the beaten egg yolks, flour and salt.
Blend slowly into hot half and half.
When thoroughly blended, pour over hot lima beans.
Stir and allow to simmer a minute or so, but do not boil.
Add and mix in snipped parsley and remove from heat.
Sprinkle with a bit of paprika if desired.
Serves 6

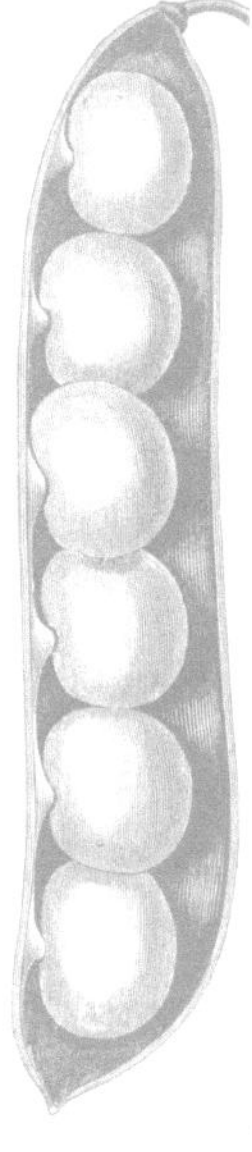

Country Style Lima Beans

4 cups fresh green lima beans
2 tablespoons butter
¾ teaspoon salt
2 teaspoons sugar
light sprinkle of pepper
¾ cup half and half

Wash lima beans several times in fresh water
to remove any grit or shell. Put beans in cooking pan.
Cover with boiling water. Add salt, sugar and pepper.
Bring to a boil and then cut back heat
and simmer beans 15-20 minutes. Turn up heat.
Bring beans to a boil and boil them until all the water has evaporated.
Watch very carefully so the beans do not burn.
Cut heat, add half and half.
Turn up heat for a second or two until the half and half
has heated but not boiled.
In corn season you might want to add a cup of fresh sweet corn.
Serves 6

Delicious Sweet Potatoes

3 cups cooked, mashed sweet potatoes
2 tablespoons Karo's Golden Syrup
1 tablespoon butter
2 tablespoons light brown sugar
½ teaspoon ground cinnamon
½ cup finely broken pecans

Mash sweet potatoes in mixing bowl until nice and smooth.
Heat Karo Syrup and butter together.
Pour over sweet potatoes and mix well.
Pour mixture into baking dish.
Mix together brown sugar, cinnamon and pecans.
Sprinkle sugar, etc. generously over sweet potatoes.
Bake in 350° oven about 30 minutes and
potatoes are lightly browned.
Serves 4-6

Sweet Potatoes Divine

3 cups cooked, mashed sweet potatoes
milk or half and half
¾ cup maple syrup
⅓ cup butter
¾ cup graham crackers crumbs
¾ teaspoon ground cinnamon
1 teaspoon light brown sugar

Mash sweet potatoes in mixer, add enough milk or half and half to make them light and fluffy, season to taste with salt and pepper.
Melt and heat together butter and maple syrup.
Pour over sweet potatoes and mix well.
Pour sweet potato mix into buttered casserole.
Mix together Graham crackers and cinnamon and about one teaspoon of brown sugar.
Sprinkle mixture generously over sweet potatoes.
Bake in 350° oven 25-30 minutes.
Serves about 6

Make-Ahead Mashed Potatoes

2½ pounds potatoes (about 5 medium size)
1 cup sour cream
4 ounces cream cheese
½ stick butter or margarine
Salt and pepper to taste

Pare and cook potatoes in lightly salted water.
Bring them to boiling and reduce heat. Cook them covered.
When done, drain potatoes and put them in mixing bowl.
Beat them until they are well mashed.
Add butter, sour cream and cream cheese.
Beat well after each addition. Add salt and pepper if desired.
Add a bit more butter, sour cream, or cream cheese if needed
to make the potatoes nice and fluffy.
Serve at once or if you wish to serve them at a later date,
spoon them into a buttered casserole. Refrigerate them until needed.
Heat them in a 350° oven until they are nice and hot
and ready to serve. The recipe may be doubled.
They are a nice make-ahead dish for holidays
or expected company.
Serves 4-6

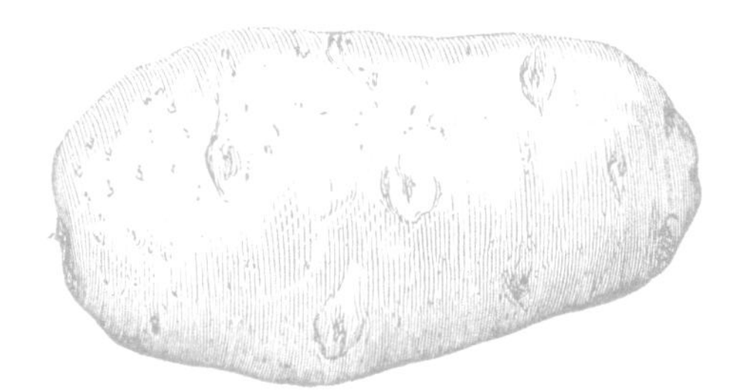

Tasty Corn Bake

2 tablespoons butter or margarine
1 (8-ounce) package cream cheese
2 (16-ounce) cans whole kernel sweet corn
½ cup red or green sweet Bell pepper, minced
¼ cup milk
½ teaspoon salt
½ teaspoon garlic salt
¼ cup Parmesan cheese
1 cup buttered bread crumbs, soft and shredded
dash or so Tabasco sauce

Melt butter or margarine and beat with cream cheese in mixer.
Add sweet corn, pepper, milk and seasonings.
Pour into buttered casserole.
Top with buttered crumbs to which has been added
the Parmesan cheese.
Bake uncovered in 325-350-degree oven until nice and bubbly.
Do not over bake.
Serves 4-6

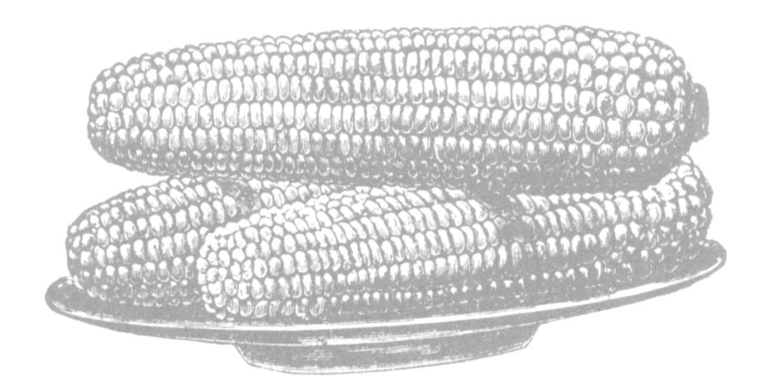

Homemade French Fries

potatoes
frying oil
salt

Peeled or unpeeled potatoes (scrubbed well).
Cut potato into ¼-inch slices. Cut the slices into ¼-inch strips.
Wash and soak strips in cold salted water about one hour.
Drain them in a colander. Spread drained strips on paper towels.
Cover with paper towels. Pat them with towels until they are dry.
Heat cooking oil in straight-sided pan.
The oil or fat should be about 375 degrees or cube of bread dropped
in hot fat should brown in about 20-25 seconds.
A wire basket is ideal to use or a slotted spoon
to lower potatoes into hot fat.
Be careful not to add too many at a time as the fat
has a tendency to boil up when the potatoes are added.
Turn potatoes that they may cook equally on each side.
When browned, lift the potatoes carefully out of the fat
and drain on paper towels. Repeat process with rest of potatoes.
This same procedure may be used for potato chips if you have a slicer
to slice them paper thin. Sprinkle fries with salt if desired.
A small bowl of ketchup on the side is nice.
It may take a couple times making to get the hang of it!
Your family will love you!

Mashed Potatoes

5-6 medium-size potatoes
½ stick butter or margarine
½ cup hot milk
salt and pepper to taste

Cook pared potatoes in slightly salted water
until they are done and remove from water.
You may use a large slotted spoon for this or drain them in a colander.
The "potato water" can be saved and refrigerated
to be used in soup or even casseroles.
Place the cooked potatoes in a mixing bowl on low speed and mash.
Add the butter and hot milk slowly.
Once they are well blended the speed may be increased.
If the potatoes seem too stiff, add a bit more butter and hot milk.
Add a bit of salt if needed and pepper.
Beat until the potatoes are light and fluffy.
Serves 6

*Sweet potatoes may be prepared the same way.
Add to sweet potatoes a little light-brown sugar
and ground cinnamon to taste.

Carrot Soufflé

3 tablespoons butter
3 tablespoons flour
1 cup hot milk
1 cup brown sugar, packed
3 eggs, separated
¼ teaspoon salt
3 cups cooked, drained and mashed carrots
½ to ¾ teaspoon ground ginger
finely chopped pecans

Melt butter in sauce pan. Stir in flour and blend well.
Slowly add hot milk. Stir and cook until thickened.
Beat egg yolks and add to sauce. Mix well. Stir into mashed carrots.
Add brown sugar and ginger and mix thoroughly.
Beat egg whites and salt until whites are stiff.
Fold whites into carrot mixture. Pour into buttered casserole.
Place casserole in pan of hot water in 350° oven
and bake 45-55 minutes.
Top with pecans in the last 10-15 minutes of baking.
Serves 6

(see photo page 100)

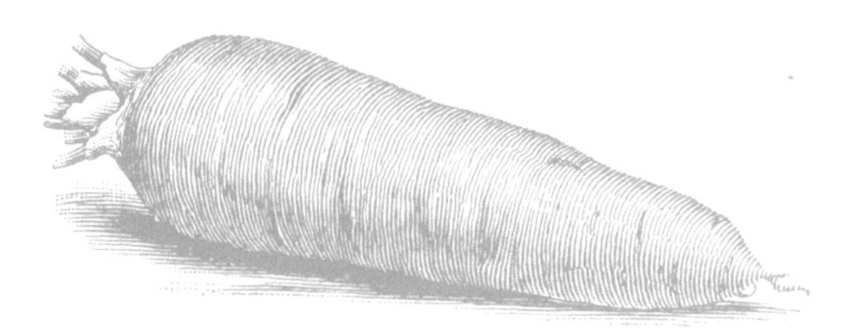

Popeye Spinach

1 10-oz package frozen spinach
2 eggs, beaten
2 tablespoons flour
½ teaspoon salt
1 cup cottage cheese
4 frankfurters cut in ¼-inch slices
2 cups shredded and buttered bread crumbs
½ cup grated Parmesan cheese
melted butter, enough to butter casserole dish and butter crumbs

Thaw spinach. Beat together eggs, flour and salt.
Mix together spinach, beaten eggs, flour and salt.
Add frankfurter slices and cottage cheese.
Pour into buttered casserole dish.
Mix together buttered bread crumbs and Parmesan cheese.
Cover top of casserole with crumbs.
Bake in 325-350° oven until ingredients are set
and crumbs crispy and lightly browned, about 45 minutes.
Serves 6

Baked Crumbs Cauliflower in Cheese Sauce

4 cups cauliflower, cut in small pieces
4 tablespoons butter
2 tablespoons flour
2 cups milk
salt and pepper to taste
1 ½ cups shredded Cheddar cheese
1 ½ cups shredded and buttered bread crumbs

Wash cauliflower and cut flowerets into small pieces.
Put into buttered casserole. Melt butter in sauce pan,
add flour, blend well on low heat.
Add milk slowly stirring and blending sauce.
Add salt and pepper to taste. Stir and add shredded cheese
until sauce is nice and smooth. Pour the hot sauce over cauliflower.
Mix well. To make coarse crumbs shred bread slices
or leftover rolls into coarse pieces and mix them generously
with melted butter or margarine.
Cover cauliflower and sauce with buttered crumbs.
Bake in 350° oven 45 minutes for a shallow dish, or 55 minutes
for a deep casserole. Check cauliflower for doneness.
The crumbs should be a golden brown.
Serves 6.

Parsnips

4 cups cooked and diced or sliced parsnips
¼ cup melted butter
½ cup light brown sugar
1 teaspoon dry mustard

Wash and scrape light skin from parsnips,
much as you would with carrots. Cook in lightly salted water.
Bring to boil and then simmer covered until parsnips are tender.
Dice or slice parsnips. Place in lightly buttered baking dish.
Drizzle evenly with melted butter.
Mix brown sugar and dry mustard together.
Sprinkle evenly over buttered parsnips.
Cover and bake in 375 degree oven about 20 minutes.
The cooked parsnips may also be served plain.
Sprinkle lightly with salt if needed, a bit of pepper,
and toss with melted butter.
Serves 4-6

Asparagus Au Gratin

3 cups fresh asparagus cut in ¾" pieces
4 tablespoons butter
2 tablespoons flour
2 cups milk
¾ cup shredded American or sharp Cheddar cheese
¼ teaspoon salt
1 cup coarsely shredded bread crumbs
Melted butter for bread crumbs

Cook asparagus in lightly salted water about 5 minutes. Drain.
Melt butter in saucepan. Add flour and blend well.
Add milk slowly, stirring constantly until sauce thickens.
Add cheese and simmer until cheese is completely blended.
Mix asparagus and cheese sauce together.
Pour into buttered baking dish.
Cover casserole with the shredded and well buttered bread crumbs.
Bake uncovered in 325° oven about 30 minutes.
Serves 6-8

Baked Fresh Tomatoes

8-10 (½" thick) fresh tomato slices
¾ cup lightly buttered fine bread crumbs
3 tablespoons Parmesan cheese
¾ teaspoon garlic salt
½ teaspoon crushed oregano leaves
¾ teaspoon crushed basil leaves
Several sprinkles garlic pepper

Mix together buttered bread crumbs
and the rest of the dry ingredients.
Pat on each slice of tomato generously on both sides.
Place in buttered baking dish or pan. Heat oven to 350 degrees.
Place pan of tomatoes on the top rack and
bake about 5 minutes or until lightly browned.
Lower dish to middle oven rack and bake another 15-20 minutes
until tomatoes are well done but not overdone.
The tomatoes may be served as a main dish or
used to garnish roast beef.
Bread crumbs may be seasoned to your taste and
any leftover crumbs may be stored in freezer
and used at a later time.
Yield 8-10 slices

Succotash

2 cups green peas
2 cups whole kernel corn
2 cups stewed chopped tomatoes and juice
3 tablespoons butter
1 tablespoon cornstarch or flour
Salt, pepper and sugar to taste

Combine butter, peas, corn, and tomatoes and juice in saucepan or kettle.
Bring to boil and stir to avoid burning. Add seasonings.
Reduce heat and simmer until vegetables are done.
Adjust seasonings to taste.
Blend cornstarch or flour in ½ cup tomato liquid that has been set aside.
Stir and blend cornstarch or flour and tomato juice with vegetables until mixture thickens.
Canned vegetables may be used, but fresh or frozen vegetables are best.
Mashed potatoes or brown buttered noodles go well with this dish.
Serves 6

Vegetarian Green Beans

2 tablespoons butter
2 tablespoons flour
½ cup finely minced onion
1 or 2 tablespoon parsley minced
A light sprinkle of vinegar or lemon juice
1 cup sour cream or cream of mushroom soup
5 cups green beans (cooked and drained)
½ cup shredded and buttered bread crumbs
½ cup shredded sharp Cheddar cheese

Sauté onion and parsley in butter. Add flour and blend.
Add sour cream or mushroom soup and blend all well.
Add sprinkle of vinegar or lemon juice and
a bit of salt and pepper if you deem it necessary.
Fold beans and parsley into mixture and blend well.
Pour into buttered 9″ x 13″ casserole.
Cover with bread crumbs and cheese
which have been mixed together.
Bake in 350-degree oven 40 minutes and crumbs
have become crisp and are lightly browned.
Serves 6

(see photo page 161)

Baked Eggplant

1 medium-size eggplant
1 egg beaten with 2 tablespoons water
Yellow corn meal or buttered bread crumbs
2 tablespoons bacon drippings or melted butter
1 diced green pepper
1 minced medium-size onion
1 cup crushed or pureed tomatoes
1½ tablespoons Worcestershire sauce
2 teaspoons sugar
Salt and pepper to taste
Parmesan cheese

Wash and pare eggplant. Cut one thin slice off top of eggplant.
Dice and set aside. Cut two one-inch crosswise slices off eggplant.
Dip one slice in bread crumbs or corn meal and then
in egg mixture and again in bread crumbs or corn meal.
Repeat with second slice. Place slices in hot drippings or butter
and fry on both sides until lightly browned.
Place one fried slice in buttered baking dish.
Sprinkle with ⅓ of the pepper and onion.
Mix together tomatoes, Worcestershire sauce, sugar,
salt, if needed, and pepper.
Drizzle two tablespoonfuls over green pepper and onion.
Sprinkle lightly with Parmesan cheese.
Place second slice over peppers, etc.
Mix remaining tomatoes, eggplant bits, green pepper,
onions, etc. and spoon over second slice.
Sprinkle lightly with Parmesan cheese.
Bake in 350 degree oven 40-45 minutes.
Serves 4-6

Stuffed Eggplant

1 fresh firm eggplant
1 cup small fresh mushrooms, sliced
½ cup minced onion
4 tablespoons melted butter
1 cup ground beef or cooked, diced ham
⅔ cup crushed or puréed tomatoes
½ teaspoon salt
2 teaspoons sugar
Dash of Tabasco sauce
Parmesan cheese

Wash, dry and peel eggplant.
Cut a slice from the top of the eggplant and scoop out the pulp, leaving about a ¼″ shell. Sauté the ground beef in the butter.
Add onion, mushrooms and eggplant pulp that has been finely chopped.
Add salt and dash of Tabasco sauce, and tomatoes to which the sugar has been added.
If using ham instead of ground beef, add it at this time.
Let onion, mushrooms, etc. simmer briefly.
Place eggplant shell in buttered baking dish.
Fill shell with tomato/meat mixture.
If shell will not hold it all, spoon it around base of shell.
Sprinkle all lightly with Parmesan cheese.
Place in 400 degree oven and bake about 20 minutes or until it is heated through and lightly browned.
Garnish with pimento bits, parsley or green pepper strips.
Mashed potatoes go well with this dish.
Serves 4-6

Collard Greens

1 pound collard greens
6-7 slices bacon
Melted butter
Salt and pepper to taste

Wash and chop collard greens coarsely.
Cook in a small amount of lightly salted and peppered water until tender. Drain well. Sauté bacon slices until crisp and brown.
Toss greens in small amount of melted butter and crisp bacon.
Serve hot. Have a cruet of vinegar handy for those who like to sprinkle a bit on the greens.
Serves 4

Collards may also be cooked and tossed with a bit of butter and bacon pieces. They may then be mixed with an equal amount of mashed potatoes and baked in a lightly buttered casserole in a 350° oven for 20-25 minutes.

Another way to prepare the greens.
Cook greens in seasoned water, drain, and toss with butter and bacon pieces. Blend together 1½ cups cream of mushroom soup and ¾ cup milk. Pour over and mix with greens.
Bake in 350 degree oven about 25-30 minutes.

Collard greens are very rich in vitamins A and C.
They may also be cooked in a mild ham broth with bits of ham added if you wish. Simmer greens until tender.
Have a cruet of vinegar handy. A side dish of mashed or fried potatoes is a nice accompanying dish.

No matter your stature,

in difficult situations,

you can always stand tall.

Cakes & Cookies

Brown Sugar Cinnamon Cookies

1 cup dark-brown sugar (packed)
2 egg whites
3 tablespoons flour
¼ teaspoon salt
¾ teaspoon ground cinnamon
½ teaspoon vanilla
2 cups finely chopped pecans

Sift brown sugar, cinnamon and flour together.
Beat egg whites and salt together until whites are stiff.
Fold in vanilla, add pecan meats. Mix all together well.
Drop by scant teaspoonfuls onto greased cookie sheet.
Bake in 350° oven 10-12 minutes.
Makes about 3 dozen.

Coconut-Almond Macaroons

½ cup + 1 tablespoon sugar
½ cup + 1 tablespoon confectioner's sugar
2 tablespoons cake flour
4 egg whites
⅔ cup crushed or ground blanched almonds
½ teaspoon vanilla or almond extract
2 cups shredded coconut

Sift together the two kinds of sugar and cake flour.
In mixer, beat egg whites until they are foamy.
Continue beating and add mixed sugar and flour,
one tablespoon at a time, beating well after each addition.
Add vanilla or almond extract.
Carefully fold in crushed almonds and coconut.
(I generally roll coconut with a rolling pin or
crush it a bit to break into smaller bits.)
When all ingredients are well mixed, drop it by teaspoon
onto brown or wax paper covered cookie sheet.
Bake 20-25 minutes in a 350° oven.
Yield 35-40 macaroons.

Old-Fashioned Mincemeat Cookies

½ cup sugar (light brown packed or white)
½ stick real butter
1 egg
1 cup canned mincemeat
1¼ cups all-purpose flour
1½ teaspoons baking powder

Beat butter in mixer. Slowly add sugar (I prefer brown).
When sugar and butter are nice and fluffy, beat in egg.
Sift together flour and baking powder.
Alternating mincemeat and flour mix, fold into butter, sugar, egg mixture. Mix all together well.
Drop batter onto well-greased cookie sheet by teaspoonfuls.
These cookies should not be baked on a thin cookie sheet as they brown easily on the bottoms.
Bake at 375-400° about 10 minutes.
They are a good soft cookie, ideal for the holidays.
Makes about 50 cookies.

Cornflake Macaroons

2 egg whites
⅛ teaspoon salt
1 cup sugar
½ teaspoon vanilla or almond extract
2 cups lightly crushed cornflakes
1 cup finely chopped pecans or English walnuts

Add salt to egg whites and beat until they are well whipped but not dry. Slowly add sugar to whites, a tablespoonful at a time. Beat well between each addition.
When all the sugar has been blended in, add extract.
Scrape sides of bowl and fold in cornflakes and nut meats.
Again scrape sides of bowl and make batter as smooth as possible.
Drop batter by teaspoonfuls onto well-greased cookie sheet.
Bake in a 350° oven 15-20 minutes or until macaroons feel firm to the touch.
When done, remove cookie sheet from oven and remove cookies from baking sheet right away.
Makes about 50 macaroons.

Lemon Wafers

⅓ cup shortening
1 cup sugar
1 egg well-beaten
2 teaspoons lemon juice
1 teaspoon grated lemon rind
¼ cup milk
2 cups cake flour
2 teaspoons baking powder
½ teaspoon salt

Cream shortening and sugar well. Add well-beaten egg.
Scrape sides of mixing bowl. Add lemon juice and lemon rind.
Mix all together well. Add ¼ cup of milk.
Sift together flour, baking powder and salt.
Add flour mix, a tablespoon or so at a time. Stir after each addition.
Scrape sides of mixing bowl again and blend mixture thoroughly.
Drop onto greased cookie sheet, ½ teaspoon at a time,
allowing about 2 inches between each cookie.
Bake in a 350° oven for 15-20 minutes
until the edges around the cookie are lightly browned
and the cookie seems to be firm on top.
Remove from cookie sheet carefully with a thin-edged spatula.
Makes 75-80.

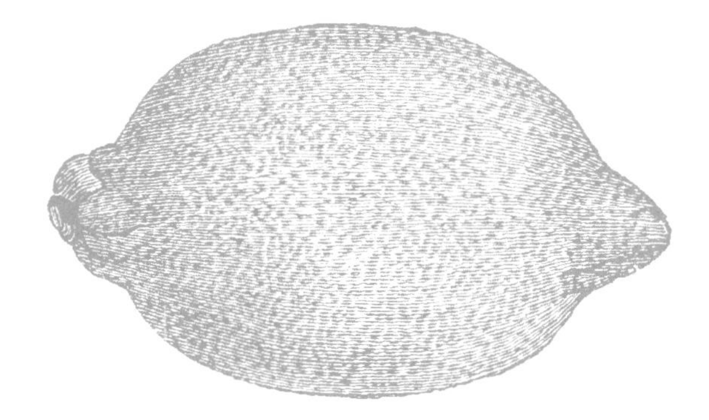

Quick Coffee Cake

2½ cups cake flour
4 teaspoons baking powder
½ teaspoon salt
⅓ cup Crisco shortening
⅓ cup sugar
1 egg
1 cup milk
½ cup seedless raisins
¼ cup chopped pecans
½ cup sugar mixed with ¼ teaspoon cinnamon

Sift together flour, baking powder and salt.
Beat shortening in mixer. Add sugar and cream well.
Add egg and blend well.
Add milk and flour, alternating, and blend well
between each addition. Fold in raisins and pecans.
Pour into well-greased and floured 9 x 9-inch baking pan.
Sprinkle mixed sugar and cinnamon generously over batter.
If you like, drizzle top with a tablespoon or so of melted butter.
Bake in 375-400° oven 25-30 minutes. Serve hot.
It can also be baked in 3, 7½ x 4-inch loaf pans.
It may be frozen and then heated and served at a later date.

Ye Olde Sugar Crisps

⅓ cup shortening
¾ cup sugar
1 egg, beaten
⅔ cup molasses
½ teaspoon vanilla
2½ cups cake flour
1 teaspoon baking powder
½ teaspoon baking soda
½ teaspoon salt
2 teaspoons ground cinnamon

Cream together shortening and sugar.
Add beaten egg, molasses and vanilla.
Cream all together well. Sift all other dry ingredients together.
Slowly add them to egg, sugar, shortening, etc.
Mix all together well.
Scrape sides of mixing bowl and blend in to cookie mix.
Drop dough by scant ½ teaspoon or less
onto well-greased cooking sheet.
Flatten cookies with greased glass bottom
that has been dipped into sugar.
Allow about a 2-inch space between each cookie.
Bake in 350-degree oven about 12-14 minutes.
Makes about 6 dozen cookies.

Fresh Coconut Cake

1 recipe of your favorite white or yellow cake or you may use a white or yellow cake mix
1 recipe Cream Cheese Frosting or Butter Cream Frosting
2 (6 oz) packages of fresh frozen coconut or fresh grated

Remove coconut from freezer and let it thaw completely in bowl on counter. Bake cake according to recipe in either loaf pan or two nine-inch layer pans. When cake is done, remove from oven. Remove loaf or layers from pans and cool completely on rack. Frost with either the Cream Cheese or Butter Frosting. Cover generously with thawed coconut. Store in cool place until serving time.
See pages 138 and 139 for frosting recipes.

***I have a customer who has had me make this cake for her each year of the last 20 or 25 years for Christmas. It has become one of their family traditions for Christmas dinner.*

In years' past one had to buy a large coconut, break it (which wasn't easy), and pour off the coconut milk. Then one peeled the broken pieces of the coconut, removing its brown skin. The peeled pieces of coconut were then grated with a little handy-dandy grater. There was an art to that, too, as one might nip a finger or two. My how times have changed.

Cream Cheese Frosting

2 (3 oz) packages cream cheese
½ cup softened butter or margarine
4½-4¾ cups confectioners sugar
2 teaspoons vanilla

Cream together cream cheese and either butter or margarine.
Add vanilla and beat until light and fluffy.
Add sugar, a little at a time, until of right consistency to spread.
Will frost top and two layers of 9-inch cake.

Butter Frosting

⅓ cup butter or margarine
4½ cups confectioners sugar
¾ cup milk
1½ teaspoons vanilla
extra milk if needed

Cream butter or margarine until light and fluffy.
Add confectioners sugar, little at a time. Add vanilla.
Beat well after each addition. Slowly add a little milk at a time.
Add milk and sugar alternating them
until of right consistency to spread.
Will frost one two-layer cake on top and sides.

Black Walnut Cake

2 cups sifted all-purpose flour
2¾ teaspoons baking powder
⅓ teaspoon salt
⅔ cup Crisco shortening (not oil)
1½ cups sugar
1 teaspoon vanilla
3 eggs, separated
¾ cup milk
1½ cups black walnut meats, finely chopped

Sift flour, baking powder, and salt together.
Put shortening in mixing bowl.
Cream shortening, add sugar and vanilla together until nice and fluffy.
Scrape sides of bowl. Add egg yolks and beat well.
When well blended, add sifted dry ingredients alternately with milk.
Scrape sides of bowl and blend all together well.
In another bowl, beat egg whites until they are stiff but not dry.
Fold whites into cake batter and mix well. Fold in nut meats.
Turn into two 9-inch greased and floured cake pans.
Bake in 350° oven about 30 minutes. Test with pick for doneness.
When done, remove from oven and cake pan.
Cool on wire rack. Decorate with your favorite frosting.
I use Cream Cheese Frosting with a few walnut meats added to frosting.

BASIC CREAM CHEESE FROSTING

6 oz cream cheese
½cup butter
4½ to 4¾ cups confectioner's sugar
2 teaspoon vanilla

(see photo page 162)

Surprise Pound Cake

2 sticks real butter
3 cups sugar
6 eggs
1 teaspoon vanilla
1 cup sour cream
3 cups flour
¼ teaspoon baking soda
¼ teaspoon salt
½ cup sliced almonds
⅓ cup maraschino cherries (quartered)

Grease a 10-inch tube cake pan.
Place small lining of waxed paper to fit bottom of pan.
Grease waxed paper. Have all ingredients at room temperature.
Sift together flour, salt, and baking soda.
Cream butter well, add sugar, adding a little at a time
and beating well after each addition.
Beat in eggs, one at a time, beating well each time.
Scrape sides of mixing bowl well, add vanilla.
Add sour cream and flour mixture, alternating them and
beating well after each addition.
Scrape sides of mixing bowl again and mix again.
Fold in almonds and cherries.
Blending all ingredients well is very important when making this cake.
Pour batter into prepared pan.
Bake in 325-degree oven about 1 hour and 20 minutes.
Test with wooden pick for doneness.
I generally cut back to 320 degrees for the last fifteen minutes.
When done, remove from oven and set pan on rack.
Allow to cool about 15 minutes. Remove from pan and cool on rack.
Dust with 10X sugar if desired.
Serves about 20-25 slices depending on size.
Freezes well.

Nut Gems

⅓ cup shortening
1⅓ cups light-brown sugar (packed)
2 well-beaten eggs
1⅓ cups cake flour
½ teaspoon salt
1 teaspoon baking powder
1 cup blanched and finely chopped almonds or pecans

Cream shortening. Sift brown sugar and add ⅓ cup to shortening.
Add beaten eggs to shortening and sugar mix.
Add rest of brown sugar.
Sift together flour, baking powder and salt
and slowly add them to shortening, egg, etc.
Mix until thoroughly blended. Fold in nut meats.
Drop onto greased cookie sheet, ¼ teaspoon at a time.
The cookies need to be spaced about 2 inches apart
as they spread remarkably. Bake in a 350° oven about 8 minutes.
Makes about 100 crispy, delicious little cookies.
I cannot emphasize too much the need to drop the batter
by ¼ teaspoons at a time.

Hazelnut Delights

½ pound hazelnuts
1⅓ cups packed brown sugar
3 egg whites
⅛ teaspoon salt
½ teaspoon vanilla
Granulated sugar

Grind hazelnuts in nut grinder.
Add salt to egg whites and whip the whites until stiff, but not dry.
Add brown sugar gradually and continue beating
until sugar has been blended in. Continue beating, add vanilla.
Roll batter into 1-inch balls. In a flat container of sugar,
roll balls in the sugar with spoon or fingers.
Put balls, well spaced, on greased cookie sheet.
Bake in a 350° oven about 12-15 minutes.
Makes about 3 dozen cookies.

Faith is the light that can guide us
safely through our darkest night.

Pies & Puddings

Applesauce Pudding

3 cups sweetened applesauce (to taste)
3 egg yolks
½ teaspoon lemon juice
½ teaspoon ground cinnamon
½ teaspoon grated lemon rind
½ teaspoon vanilla
3 egg whites
⅛ teaspoon salt
6 tablespoons sugar

Mix applesauce (sweetened to taste) lemon juice, cinnamon, vanilla and lemon rind, beat in egg yolks.
Pour into baking dish from which it may be served. Make meringue.
Beat egg whites, add salt, add sugar, slowly add vanilla and beat until whites will stand in soft peaks.
Cover applesauce mix with meringue, making sure the meringue touches the outer rim of baking dish.
Place baking dish of pudding in pan of water.
Preheat oven to 300° to 325° and bake pudding 15-20 minutes until meringue is golden brown.
Serve very hot or very cold.
Serves 4-5

Baked Corn Custard

2 cups canned or frozen corn
3 beaten eggs
2 teaspoons melted butter
2 cups milk
¾ teaspoon sugar
salt and pepper to taste
buttered bread or cracker crumbs

If you are using frozen corn, cook it in lightly salted, small amount of water.
Beat eggs well, and add sugar to milk and melted butter.
Mix corn with eggs and milk. Season with salt and pepper.
Pour into buttered baking dish. Cover lightly with crumbs.
Bake in 250° oven 40 minutes or until set and knife comes out clean when tested in middle of casserole.
Serves 4

Luscious Lime Pie

1 (3 ounce) package lime Jell-O
½ cup milk
8 large marshmallows
1 (3 ounce) package cream cheese (room temperature)
1 (10 ounce) can crushed pineapple
⅓ cup mayonnaise
½ cup whipping cream
1 graham cracker pie shell

Heat milk, add marshmallows, reduce heat, stir until melted.
Add cream cheese and stir until dissolved.
Add Jell-O to the hot mix. Stir until dissolved. Remove from heat.
Cool. Add crushed pineapple and mayonnaise.
Refrigerate briefly. When it begins to thicken,
beat whipping cream and fold into Jell-O mix.
Pour into prepared shell.
(I make shell ahead and bake it in 350° oven about 10 minutes or until firm and let it cool before adding pie mixture.)
The pie should be kept refrigerated until serving.
A dollop of whipped cream or Cool-Whip may serve as a garnish for each serving if desired.
The recipe may be doubled for two pies.

Butterscotch Pie

¾ cup brown sugar (packed)
¼ cup white sugar (plain)
⅓ cup flour
2 cups scalded milk
⅛ teaspoon salt
3 beaten egg yolks
1½ tablespoons butter
1 teaspoon vanilla
1 baked pastry shell
Meringue

Mix together brown and white sugar and flour.
Slowly stir in hot milk. Stir until well blended.
Add salt and pour into double boiler.
Cook slowly and stir until it has thickened.
Spoon a bit of the thick sauce into the beaten egg yolks.
Blend thoroughly and pour back into milk, etc. Stir and cook.
Add butter and stir until butter is completely melted
and blended in custard. Cool briefly, add vanilla.
Pour custard into baked pie shell. Top pie with meringue.
Be sure meringue touches inside edge of pastry shell.
Place in 325-degree oven about 15 minutes
until it is a nice golden brown.
See meringue page 150.

Meringue

3 egg whites
6 tablespoons sugar
½ teaspoon vanilla
¼ teaspoon cream of tartar

Place egg whites in mixing bowl.
The egg whites should be at room temperature.
Add cream of tartar and vanilla.
Beat on medium speed about one minute or so.
Increase to high speed and gradually add sugar, one tablespoon
at a time until all the sugar has been used
and whites are glossy and will peak well, but not dry.
Scrape sides of bowl and blend all in. Top pie with meringue.
Place in 325-degree oven and bake
until meringue is a nice light brown.
Remove pie from oven and let cool on a rack.
Refrigerate until serving time.
Serves 6-8

Pineapple Custard Pie

¾ cup sugar
1 cup finely crushed and drained pineapple
1 mashed banana (optional)
1 cup milk
2 tablespoons cornstarch
3 egg yolks, beaten
3 egg whites
1 baked pie shell

Mix cornstarch and sugar together. Blend in milk. Place in double boiler. Slowly add beaten egg yolks. Cook all together until it thickens. Remove from heat. Fold in well-drained pineapple and banana (if using), then fold in beaten egg whites.
Mix all together well and pour into baked pie shell. When cold, cover with sweetened whipped cream or a dollop on each slice at serving time.
Serves 6-8

Mincemeat-Apple Bake

4 slices cinnamon or cinnamon raisin bread
3 tablespoons melted butter or margarine
2 tablespoons white or light-brown sugar
½ teaspoon ground cinnamon
1½ cups canned mincemeat
⅓ cup chopped pecans
1½ cups diced apples

Shred bread slices and toss with 2 tablespoons of the butter.
Add the sugar and ground cinnamon.
Butter a 1½ quart baking dish with remaining butter.
Mix together the mincemeat and apples.
Line the baking dish with half of the crumb mix.
Pour mincemeat and apples into baking dish.
Add pecans to remaining crumbs and
sprinkle overtop the apple-mincemeat mix.
Bake in 325° oven 30-35 minutes.
Serves 6

This dish goes quite well with pork or beef roasts.

Vegetarian Green Beans
page 132

Black Walnut Cake

page 148

Beef Roast and Red Potatoes
page 91

Old Fashion Corn Bread
page 179

Fruit Bowl or Tray
page 215

No-Bake Rice Pudding

½ cup rice
1 cup water
½ teaspoon salt
½ stick butter or margarine
4 cups milk
½ cup sugar
1 teaspoon vanilla
½ teaspoon ground cinnamon (optional)
2 beaten eggs
1 cup seedless raisins

Rinse raisins and soak them in water about 25-30 minutes.
Cook rice in water with salt.
When it starts to thicken, add butter or margarine.
Add milk slowly and cook until the rice thickens
and is just about done. This will take 45 minutes to one hour.
Remove from heat and add the beaten eggs, vanilla,
and cinnamon if desired. Mix well until all is nicely blended.
Add drained raisins, return to heat, stir
and simmer a few minutes until pudding is nice and thick.
Remove from heat, cool a bit and serve warm
or refrigerate until needed to serve.
Serves 6-8

Old-Fashioned Rice Custard

½ cup light brown sugar (packed)
2 cups cooked rice
3 tablespoons melted butter
1 cup milk, heated
3 eggs, slightly beaten
½ cup seedless raisins
½ teaspoon vanilla
dash of nutmeg

Place rice, sugar, melted butter, heated milk in large bowl.
(The rice should have been cooked in lightly salted water.)
Add lightly beaten eggs. Mix all together well.
Pour into casserole or deep baking dish.
Bake at 350° oven about one hour.
When baking time is half gone, remove from oven
and stir in raisins and vanilla and sprinkle
top with the ground nutmeg.
Replace in oven and bake for the rest of the baking time
or until custard is done.
Serves 6

Grandma's Baked Custard

3 large eggs
¼ teaspoon salt
⅓ cup sugar
3 cups scalded milk
½ teaspoon vanilla or almond extract
ground nutmeg or cinnamon

Beat eggs until whites and yolks are well blended, but do not over beat. Add sugar and salt to eggs and blend well. Add the vanilla or almond extract.
Pour scalded milk into egg mixture, a small amount at a time, mixing as you go. When all milk has been blended in, pour into custard cups or a shallow baking dish.
Sprinkle the nutmeg or cinnamon on top of the liquid.
Set in pan of hot water in the oven and bake at 350° about 35-40 minutes, depending on depth of liquid in the containers.
Test for doneness with a knife blade, inserting it in the center of the custard. If it comes out clean, the custard is done.
Makes about 4-6 servings.

Orange Pineapple Mallow Pie

1 (3 oz) package orange Jell-o
8 large marshmallows
3 oz cream cheese
½ cup milk
½ cup crushed pineapple
½ cup diced mandarin oranges
⅓ cup mayonnaise
½ cup whipping cream
1 prepared graham cracker pie crust

Melt marshmallows in heated milk in saucepan.
Keep on low heat. Watch and stir often to keep milk
and marshmallows from scorching.
When the marshmallows are thoroughly melted,
add cream cheese and stir until it is completely dissolved.
Stir Jell-o into hot mixture. Set aside to cool.
When completely cooled, add pineapple and mandarin oranges.
Set in cold place to chill. When mixture begins to set,
whip cream and add it to chilled mixture.
Stir and fold all together well. Pour mixture into prepared shell.
When nicely set, decorate with mandarin orange slices,
whipped cream or dollops of commercial whipped topping.
Keep chilled until ready to serve.
Serves 8.

Fruit Pie Deluxe

1½ cups diced canned peach slices
1½ cups crushed pineapple
¾ cup sugar
¼ cup flour
1 (3 oz) package orange Jell-O
3 bananas (sliced)
½ cup chopped pecans or English walnuts
2 (8-inch) or 1 (10-inch) baked pie shell or shells
slightly sweetened whipped cream, ice cream or whipped topping

Combine peaches, pineapple, sugar and flour
and cook until it thickens. Add orange Jell-O.
Stir until it dissolves. Set aside to cool.
When mixture becomes lukewarm or cooler, add bananas and nuts.
Pour into baked pie shell or shells.
Decorate with peach or banana slices if desired.
Serve with a dollop of whipped cream, ice cream,
or whipped topping. Refrigerate until served.
Serves 8

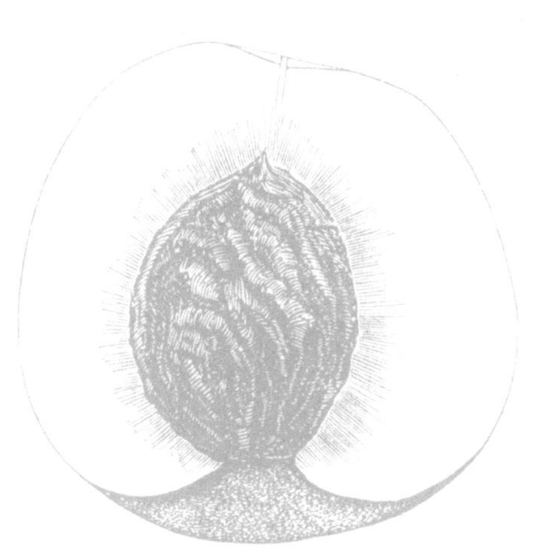

Maple Nut Pudding

⅓ cup cornstarch
¼ cup cold water
1½ cups packed light-brown sugar
2 cups boiling water
3 stiffly beaten egg whites
⅓ cup chopped pecans or English walnuts

Mix cornstarch and cold water together.
Stir until cornstarch is completely dissolved.
Add 1½ cups packed brown sugar and 2 cups boiling water.
Cook until mixture thickens stirring often.
Place pan with cornstarch, water, and sugar over the bottom of a double boiler and cook 20 minutes or until it is thick.
Stir frequently. Remove from heat and cool until it becomes lukewarm. Add stiffly beaten egg whites and nut meats. Fold in and blend all together.
Pour into individual sherbet or dessert dishes.
Chill well in refrigerator until ready to serve.
A small dollop of ice cream or whipped cream adds a nice touch.
Makes 6-8 servings.

Easy Lemon Pie

1 (3 oz) package lemon Jell-O
1 cup boiling water
Juice and grated rind of one lemon
½ cup sugar
1 (12 oz) can Pet Evaporated Milk (chilled)
2 prepared graham cracker pie shells

Graham Cracker Shell Mix
2½ cups graham cracker crumbs
½ cup sugar
⅔ cup softened butter or margarine

This recipe will make two 9-inch crusts and garnish for top of 2 (9-inch) pies or 1 deep (10-inch) pie.

Dissolve package of lemon Jell-O in the cup of boiling water. Let it set until it is well dissolved. Set aside to cool. When well cooled, mix together lemon juice, rind, and sugar. In electric mixer, beat the well chilled evaporated milk until it is the consistency of whipped cream. Fold the whipped milk into the Jell-O, lemon juice, rind and sugar. When all ingredients are well blended, pour filling into prepared pie shell or shells. Sprinkle generously with prepared graham cracker crumbs. Refrigerate until ready to serve.

This recipe may also be used in other ways. Pour filling into sherbets and sprinkle with crumbs. The filling may also be poured into a crumb-lined square or rectangular Pyrex casserole. Cover with graham cracker crumbs. Chilled and cut into squares and topped with a dollop of whipped topping for individual desserts.

Luscious Fruit Salad Pie

1 ¼ cups canned sliced peaches
1 ¼ cups crushed pineapple
¾ cup sugar (½ cup if peaches were in heavy syrup)
¼ cup flour
1 (3 ounce) package orange Jell-O
2 sliced bananas (not overly ripe)
½ cup chopped pecans or English walnuts
1 baked pie shell
Lightly sweetened whipped cream or ice cream

Dice drained peaches and combine with crushed pineapple, sugar and flour. Mix thoroughly. Place in saucepan and cook until thickened. Remove from heat. Stir Jell-O into hot mixture and stir until it is completely dissolved. Set aside to cool. When no more than slightly warm, add bananas and nuts. Pour into baked pie shell. Garnish with extra peach slices. Refrigerate until well set. When ready to serve, top each slice with a dollop of ice cream or slightly sweetened whipped cream or commercial whipped topping if desired.

Serves 8

Peach Custard Pie

2 cups drained and diced canned peaches
¾ cup crushed pineapple
2 tablespoons cornstarch
½ cup sugar
2 slightly beaten eggs
3 ounces cream cheese (softened)
1 cup dairy sour cream
1 9" baked pie shell

Mix drained peach syrup, about 1 cup or a bit more, with cornstarch. Cook on low heat until it thickens. Remove from heat. When slightly cooled, add to it the cream cheese and sour cream that have been beaten together. Add beaten eggs and sugar. Mix until well blended. Fold and blend together with diced peaches and pineapple. Pour mixture into prepared and baked pie shell. Bake in 375 degree oven 30-35 minutes or until custard is set. Refrigerate pie until serving time. A dollop of whipped cream or commercial whipped topping can only add to its goodness.

Serves 8

Apple Raisin Pie

1½ cups seedless raisins
2 tablespoons flour
¾ cup sugar
1½ tablespoons vinegar
1 cup water
2½ cups pared and sliced apples
¼ teaspoon ground cinnamon
1 tablespoon melted butter
Pastry for top and bottom of deep 9" pie

Cook together in saucepan, raisins, sugar, flour, vinegar, cinnamon and water that have been mixed together.
Stir and cook on medium heat until slightly thickened.
Add apples and butter. Mix all together well.
Spoon into bottom of pie shell. Cover with top pastry.
Seal edges. Cut slits in top pastry. Brush top of pastry with milk and sprinkle with sugar if desired. Place pie in 450 degree oven.
Bake 10-15 minutes. Reduce heat to 350 degrees and bake another 35-40 minutes or until pie is lightly browned.
Serves 8

PASTRY

2 cups flour
1 cup Crisco shortening
1 teaspoon salt
1 egg and ice water, enough to fill 1/2 cup.
Another tablespoon or so may be needed, but add just a bit at a time, just enough to hold the dough together.

Fresh Peach Pie

5-6 ripe peaches
½–⅔ cup sugar, depending on peach ripeness
2 tablespoons flour
¼ teaspoon ground cinnamon
½ cup sour cream
Pie pastry for shell and top crust

Line pie pan with pastry. Mix first five ingredients well and spoon into pastry shell. Top with pastry. Crimp edges well. Make several slashes in pastry.
Brush pastry with milk or lightly beaten egg white.
Bake in 425 degree oven 10-15 minutes.
Reduce heat to 350° and bake another 30-35 minutes or until top is golden brown. If you prefer, you may omit top pastry. Sprinkle top of filling with ½ cup grated sharp cheese and bake as before. See page 162 for sweet pastry dough.
Pie serves 8

An angry word from a friend or loved one is just about the most painful dart of all.

Rolls, Breads & Quick Breads

Best Corn Bread

2 eggs, slightly beaten
1¼ cups milk
¼ cup melted shortening
1½ cups yellow corn meal
¾ cup sifted flour
1 teaspoon salt
2 tablespoons sugar
2½ teaspoons baking powder
Drizzle butter or bacon drippings

Add slightly beaten eggs to milk and melted shortening.
Sift together corn meal, flour, salt, sugar and baking powder.
Stir all together quickly.
Pour into buttered 1½ quart casserole or pan.
Drizzle batter with melted butter or drippings.
Bake in 400-degree oven for 20-25 minutes
until wooden pick comes out clean
and top is very lightly browned.
Serves 6

Old-Fashion Corn Bread

3 cups sifted flour
1½ cups yellow corn meal
2 tablespoons baking powder
2 tablespoons sugar
1½ teaspoon salt
½ cup melted butter or margarine
2½ cups milk
2-3 tablespoons melted butter to drizzle over batter

Grease a 9 x 9-inch baking pan.
Cover bottom with waxed paper and grease paper.
Sift flour, corn meal, baking powder, sugar and salt into large bowl.
Pour ½ cup butter into milk. Stir and pour all at once into flour,
corn meal, etc. Stir with wooden spoon, quickly blending all together.
Stir only until well blended. Pour into pan and
smooth top of batter with a few quick strokes.
Drizzle batter with melted butter or you can use bacon drippings.
Bake in 425° oven for 30-35 minutes and top is lightly browned.
This recipe is good for those who cannot eat eggs.
Serve hot. Makes 16, 2-inch squares.
Leftovers can be reheated at a later time.

(see photo page 163)

Old-Fashioned Corn Fritters

1 cup flour
1 teaspoon baking powder
½ teaspoon salt
1 egg
¼ cup milk
½ tablespoon butter, melted
1 cup crushed and drained sweet corn
Fat to fry fritters
Confectioner's sugar

Sift flour, baking powder and salt together.
Gradually add beaten egg and milk.
Pour melted butter over corn and fold into flour mix,
beaten egg and milk batter.
Drop by small spoonfuls into hot fat and fry on both sides
until nicely browned. Remove from fat and drain on paper towels.
Repeat until all batter has been used.
Sprinkle fritters with a dusting of confectioner's sugar.
Serve hot.
Makes about 18 small fritters.

Bacon Breakfast Muffins

6-8 slices bacon
1 1/4 cups flour
1 tablespoon sugar
1 teaspoon salt
1 1/2 teaspoons baking powder
1 egg
3/4 cup milk
1 tablespoon bacon drippings

Grease muffin pans. Sauté bacon and place on paper towels to absorb fat. Set aside bacon drippings from sauté pan. Crumble cooked bacon slices. Sift together flour, sugar, salt and baking powder. Beat together lightly, eggs, drippings, milk and add to crumbled bacon. Combine dry ingredients and egg, milk, bacon drippings, and bacon. Blend together quickly. Fill muffin pans about half full. Place in 450° oven and bake about 15-20 minutes. Remove from oven and serve. Makes about 16. Leftovers may be reheated in a well-covered container in a 400° oven in about 5 minutes.

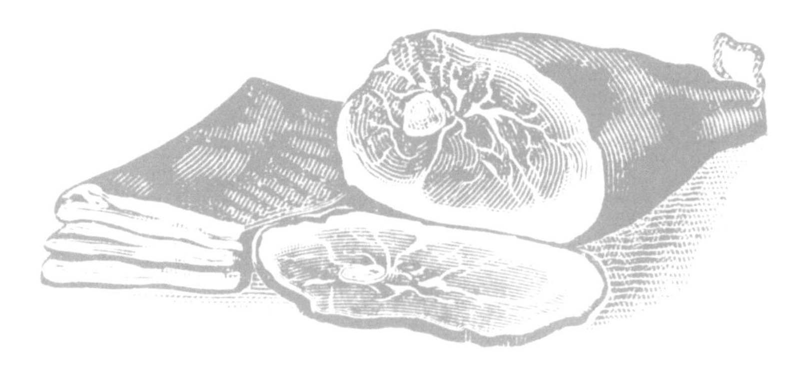

Corn Muffins

1½ cups sifted flour
2¼ teaspoons baking powder
2 tablespoons sugar
¾ teaspoon salt
¾ cup yellow corn meal
2 eggs, lightly beaten
1 cup milk
4 tablespoons melted butter

Sift flour, baking powder, salt and sugar together twice.
Add corn meal and sift again. Combine eggs, milk and melted butter.
Add milk, etc. to sifted dry ingredients.
Stir only long enough to blend all together.
Spoon into well-greased muffin pans/tins. Fill ½ full.
Bake in 425° oven for 25 minutes. Serve hot.
Extras may be reheated at a later date. The secret of good muffins is to not over beat or stir batter. The quicker they can be blended together, the better.
This recipe makes 12-16 muffins.

Bacon Cornbread Muffins

1 cup corn meal
1 cup flour
2 tablespoons sugar
½ cup sautéed and crumbled bacon
4 teaspoons baking powder
½ teaspoon salt
1 egg
¼ cup melted shortening
1 cup milk

Mix first six ingredients together including crumbled bacon. Beat together beaten egg, melted shortening (this can be bacon drippings) and milk. Blend together quickly, stirring just enough to dampen all ingredients well. Spoon into greased muffin cups. Fill about ⅔ full. Bake in 400-degree oven about 25 minutes. Makes 12-15 muffins.

Old-Fashioned Spoon Bread

4 slices bacon, sautéed and crumbled
3 ½ cups milk
1 cup yellow corn meal
2 eggs, beaten
3 tablespoons butter or bacon drippings
3 tablespoons sugar
¼ teaspoon salt

Blend together corn meal and milk.
Stir and cook together on low heat until it thickens.
Remove from heat. Add lightly beaten eggs, bacon,
bacon drippings or butter, sugar and salt.
Pour into buttered baking dish and bake in 325° oven for one hour.
Hot essence from roast beef or baked ham
is good drizzled over it.
Serves 6

Mrs. Toms' Rolls

2 eggs
1 cup water
2 packages active dry yeast
1 ⅓ cups milk (scalded)
2 tablespoons sugar
2 tablespoons Crisco
1 ½ teaspoons salt
1 extra tablespoon sugar
about 1 ¾ pounds Gold Medal Wondra flour

Break eggs into mixer bowl, add 1 cup water.
Measure 2 tablespoons sugar, Crisco and salt into another bowl and pour the hot scalded milk over it.
Beat eggs and water and add about ⅓ of the milk mixture over eggs and water in mixer.
When lukewarm add yeast and 1 tablespoon of sugar.
Mix thoroughly. When the other ⅔ of the milk is lukewarm, add to eggs etc. and begin beating in the flour a small amount at a time. Continue adding the flour and mixing until dough seems stiff enough to handle. Turn dough out on floured board and with care, work dough into a soft ball.
Return dough into bowl, grease top lightly with melted Crisco.
Cover and set in warm place to rise. When doubled in bulk, punch down dough and using greased hands, squeeze out 1 inch little balls of dough between your thumb and fore finger.
Place little rolls on a greased baking sheet and let them rise until doubled in size.
Bake at 375° for 10-12 minutes.

Never allow your dough to get too warm or too cold.
Just nice and warm.
This recipe may be used for cinnamon buns and sticky buns.
Makes 5 dozen rolls

Corn Meal Cakes

1⅓ cups corn meal
⅔ cup flour
1 teaspoon baking soda
1½ tablespoons melted butter
1 tablespoon sugar
½ teaspoon salt
2 eggs
1½ cups sour milk or buttermilk

Sift together corn meal, flour, baking soda, sugar and salt.
Beat eggs well. Add melted butter and sour milk or buttermilk.
Pour egg mixture into corn meal, etc. mix.
Blend all together well. Pour batter into pitcher.
Heat heavy skillet or griddle. Melt fat in heated skillet or griddle.
Pour batter in hot fat from pitcher, enough to make about a 5" cake.
Brown on one side. Flip cake to other side and fry until browned.
Repeat, adding a small amount of fat after each cake.
Make as many cakes as desired.
Leftover batter may be refrigerated and used later.
Recipe makes 12-15 cakes, depending on size.
Serve hot with molasses, maple syrup, pork "puddin" or sausages.
Wonderful on a cold winter morning!

Blueberry Muffins

1¾ cups all purpose flour
¾ teaspoon salt
1/2 cup sugar
2¼ teaspoons baking powder
2 eggs
4 tablespoons melted butter or margarine
¾ cup milk
1 cup fresh blueberries
1 tablespoon flour

Sift together flour, salt, sugar and baking powder.
Beat eggs until yolks and whites are well blended and frothy.
Do not over beat. Stir together milk and melted butter.
Mix milk and butter with lightly beaten eggs.
Stir in flour, salt, sugar, and baking powder.
Blend together quickly but do not over beat.
Fold in blueberries which have been rinsed and allowed to dry,
and then dusted with the tablespoon of flour.
Fill well-greased muffin cups ⅓ to ½ full.
You may wish to use paper cups placed in greased muffin tins.
Bake at 425 degrees about 15-20 minutes
depending on depth of batter in muffin cups.
Makes about 18-20 muffins.
Muffins may be reheated, if desired,
in a tightly foil-covered, wax paper lined pan.

Bea's Kinkling Cousins

¾ cup milk
½ cup sugar
1¼ teaspoon salt
½ cup butter or margarine
⅓ cup lukewarm water
2 packages dry yeast
3 eggs (room temperature)
5-6 cups flour (I use Gold Metal Wondra flour.)
Oil for frying

Have mixing bowl, eggs, etc. at room temperature.
Scald milk, add sugar, salt and butter or margarine.
Stir until butter or margarine has melted completely.
Set aside to cool. Pour warm water in mixing bowl, add dry yeast.
Add eggs and beat all a minute or so. With mixer at low speed, add flour, a half cup or so at a time, mixing well after each addition.
Scrape sides of bowl occasionally.
Continue to add flour (no more than 6 cups) until dough clings to dough hook and draws away from sides of bowl.
Continue to mix or knead dough 6-7 minutes until it is nice and smooth.
Turn dough onto a lightly floured board and quickly form dough into a ball-like shape.
Place in lightly greased bowl. Brush top and sides of dough with melted shortening. Set in warm place to rise.
When doubled in bulk, punch down dough with greased hands.
Roll out a portion of dough to ½" thickness.
Cut circles of dough with 2¾" cookie cutter.
Dip cutter in flour between each cutting.

Place cut dough on greased cookie sheet. Place in warm place to rise.
When not quite doubled, pour frying oil 1½" deep in deep fryer.
Heat until a small cube of bread will brown in several seconds.
Carefully place cut dough in hot oil. Brown lightly on one side.
Turn and brown other side. This will take several seconds.
Do not over brown. Remove from fat and drain on paper towels.
Continue as before with remaining dough.
Dust fried "kinklings" with confectioner's sugar.
Best served immediately or can be stored or frozen and reheated.
Makes about one dozen "kinklings."

You may add ½ teaspoon ground cinnamon and/or
½ cup chopped pecans for variety if you wish.
Mix cinnamon with sugar, add pecans when about half of the flour
had been added to the soft dough.

Bea's Kinkling Teasers

Use a portion of Bea's Kinkling Cousins (above)
to make tiny "kinklings." Cut dough with ¾" cookie cutter and use
same procedure as before to make these delightful little morsels.

They say, "Life is what you make it."
Let's make it the very best we can.

Special Recipes

Hominy Cakes

2 cups canned hominy
2 small or one extra larger egg
2½ tablespoons flour
1 cup finely diced ham or 6 slices bacon, sautéed and crumbled
½ cup shredded sharp Cheddar cheese or Parmesan cheese
½ teaspoon salt (optional)
buttered bread crumbs

Mix hominy, eggs, flour, add crumbled bacon or cubed ham.
Pat into small round cakes.
Mix crumbs and cheese and pat onto and around cakes.
Cover them generously with crumbs.
Using about 2-3 tablespoons of the bacon drippings
or butter, fry slowly at medium heat until lightly browned.
Turn them over and repeat process.
When nicely browned remove from heat and serve.
There will be six or seven cakes.
These cakes are good with applesauce or syrup on the side.
Nice for breakfast or lunch.

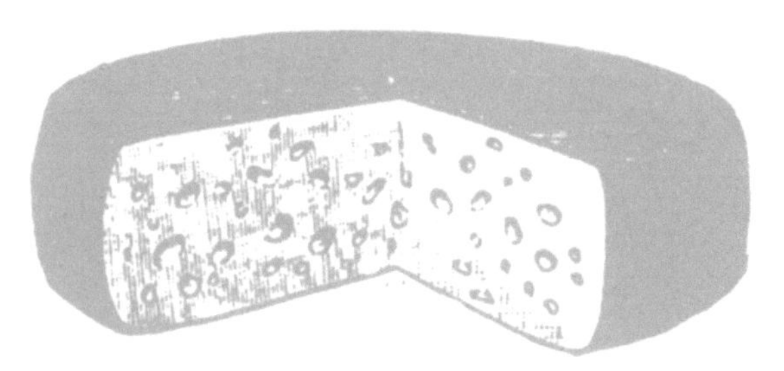

Quick Easy Chili

2½ cups cooked rice
1 tablespoon melted butter or margarine
½ cup finely minced onion
1 minced clove of garlic or ½ teaspoon garlic powder
2 level teaspoons chili powder
¾-pound lean hamburger (ground round beef)
2½ cups beef broth
2 tablespoons flour
½ cup tomato sauce
1 cup cooked red kidney beans

Sauté ground beef in melted butter.
Add minced onion and garlic or garlic powder.
Stir together beef broth, flour, tomato sauce, chili powder.
Stir and cook until it thickens.
Add kidney beans and sautéed beef, onion and garlic.
Mix all together and simmer 25-30 minutes.
Place cooked rice on large serving platter and pour chili over it.
Sprinkle with a bit of Parmesan cheese for a nice touch.
The rice and chili could also be served in separate dishes
and quantities of each dish taken at individual's pleasure.
Serves 6

Beans, Meat and Potatoes

4 cups cooked green beans, fresh, frozen, or canned
1 medium-size potato, finely diced
1 cup finely diced ham or sautéed bacon
½ cup minced onion
Dash garlic pepper

Place cooked beans and their broth in pot.
Add potatoes, ham or bacon and minced onion.
Add dash of garlic pepper. Cover lightly, bring to boil.
Reduce heat and simmer about 30 minutes
or until potatoes are well done.
Fresh beans are best and I prefer them,
but they do take a bit more time to prepare.
Hot corn bread or biscuits are nice on the side.
Serves 6

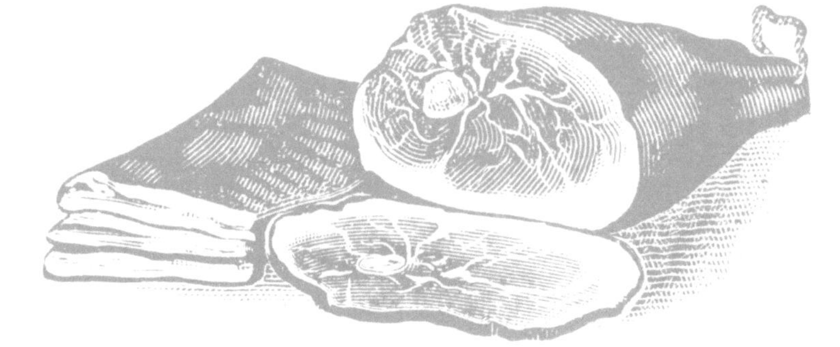

Supper in a Skillet

1 small head green cabbage
2-3 medium-size potatoes, sliced
6-8 slices smoked ham
½ cup minced onion or 2 tablespoons onion flakes
1 cup water

Wash cabbage head. Remove any unsightly leaves.
Cut cabbage head into small, even-sized wedges.
Arrange the wedges around the outer edge
of a large skillet or saucepan. Place thickly sliced potatoes in center.
Sprinkle with pepper if desired.
The dish will require little or no salt.
Cover each wedge of cabbage and the potatoes
with a thin slice of ham. Add water to pan.
Cover the pan with a tight-fitting lid. Bring contents to a boil.
Reduce heat immediately and simmer 30-35 minutes.
Check vegetables for doneness.
Serves 4.

Delicious One-Dish Dinner

1 pound ground round beef steak
2 tablespoons bacon drippings or butter
½ cup finely minced onion
1 small clove garlic, finely minced (optional)
2 cups stewed and chopped tomatoes, canned or fresh
2 cups corn, fresh or frozen
4 tablespoons melted butter or margarine
5 tablespoons flour
½ tablespoon brown sugar
2 teaspoon salt or to taste
dash or two Tabasco sauce
1½ cups shredded bread crumbs
Melted butter for crumbs

Grease or butter a baking dish.
Sauté onion and/or garlic in bacon drippings or butter.
Stir in ground beef and stir until browned.
Add the tomatoes and corn. In another pan, melt butter,
stir in flour and stir until lightly browned. Add brown sugar.
Mix together the beef, tomatoes and corn
with the flour/butter mixture.
Season to taste with salt and Tabasco sauce.
Simmer until all ingredients are blended well.
Pour all into baking dish.
Top with shredded and buttered bread crumbs.
Bake in 425° oven for 20 minutes or so and
bread crumbs are nicely browned.
I prefer using bran cereal, day-old bread or rolls as opposed
to the packaged dry crumbs for this dish.
A little grated Parmesan cheese is good mixed with the crumbs.
Serves 6

Eggs Creole

2½ cups chopped tomatoes, canned or fresh
½ cup finely minced onion
½ cup finely minced green pepper
½ cup finely chopped celery
1½ teaspoons sugar
1 cup shredded or torn bread crumbs
1½ tablespoons melted butter
4 eggs, slightly beaten
salt and pepper to taste
½ bay leaf
1 cup shredded American or sharp Cheddar cheese

Cook tomatoes, onion, green pepper, celery, sugar, and bay leaf all together about 10-15 minutes. Remove bay leaf. Add buttered bread crumbs. Mix all together and pour into buttered casserole. Beat eggs until lightly blended. Pour eggs over casserole covering tomatoes, etc. Sprinkle lightly with salt and pepper. Sprinkle shredded cheese evenly over eggs. Bake in 350° oven about 35 minutes or until eggs have set and cheese has melted well.

Serves 6-8

Corned Beef and Cabbage Supper

4 pounds corned beef
3½ to 4 pounds of cabbage
2-3 potatoes, thinly sliced
2-3 carrots, sliced diagonally
seasonings to taste

Wipe corned beef with damp cloth.
Place in a pot of cold water to cover. Bring to a boil.
If a scum appears, remove it carefully.
Sprinkle the corned beef with pepper, a little minced garlic or finely minced onion. Simmer on low heat about 2½ to 3 hours. About 20 minutes before the corned beef is done,
add the sliced potatoes and carrots.
Cut the cabbage into small wedges and cover beef and other vegetables, salt and pepper lightly, and cook covered until cabbage and other vegetables are done, about 15-20 minutes.
To serve, placed corned beef on large platter
and surround it with the vegetables.
Serves 8 generously.

Canned corned beef is also available
and saves much time in preparation. You can adjust quantities of ingredients based on size of corned beef you acquire.
If using canned corned beef, you may wish to drizzle
a little melted butter or bacon drippings over the cabbage, etc.
Hot corn bread goes well with this dish.

Red Kidney Bean Deluxe

4 cups canned kidney beans and juices
1 cup cooked rice
½ cup finely minced onion
6-8 slices sautéed and crumbled bacon
1½ cups canned or freshly chopped tomatoes
2 tablespoons brown sugar
½ cup ham or chicken broth
½ tablespoon flour
dash Tabasco sauce (optional)
2 cups buttered shredded bread crumbs
¼ cup grated Parmesan cheese

Butter bottom of a 2-qt casserole.
Sauté onions in 2 tablespoons bacon drippings.
Blend together broth (ham or chicken) flour, and brown sugar.
Mix well. Mix together beans, rice, onion, and bacon.
Add to tomatoes, flour, broth, and brown sugar mix.
Add Tabasco sauce, if desired.
Mix buttered crumbs with Parmesan cheese.
Pour bean mix into casserole. Sprinkle bread mix generously over beans, etc. Bake in 350° oven about 40-45 minutes until crumb mix is lightly browned and ingredients in casserole are set.
Dish is good with mashed potatoes and a green salad on the side.
Serves 6-8

Old-Fashioned Griddle Cakes

1 cup sifted cake flour
½ teaspoon baking soda
½ teaspoon salt
1 well beaten egg
1 tablespoon sugar
1 cup thick sour milk or butter milk
1 teaspoon melted butter

Sift flour once. Sift again with baking soda, salt and sugar.
Beat egg in a bowl. Add sour milk or buttermilk
alternating sifted dry mix and liquid. Mix into melted butter.
Blend all well. Bake on hot griddle or skillet.
Bacon drippings, butter or other fats may be used to fry cakes.
Maple syrup, corn syrup or butter are equally good with these cakes.
Small browned sausages are also enjoyable.
Yields 10-12 cakes.

Spaghetti and Sauce

1 pound hamburger
1 tablespoon butter
½ cup minced onion
1 tablespoon flour
1 (28-ounce) can tomatoes
1 teaspoon garlic salt or 1 minced garlic clove
1 teaspoon crushed basil leaves
1/8 teaspoon oregano
2½-3 teaspoons sugar
Dash of Tabasco Sauce
1 (8-ounce) package of thin spaghetti
Grated Parmesan cheese

Sauté hamburger in butter until lightly browned.
Add onions and sauté until cooked.
Puree tomatoes (I do mine in a blender.).
To the tomatoes add flour, garlic salt or minced garlic, basil leaves, oregano, sugar, dash of Tabasco and salt and pepper if needed.
Blend hamburger and tomato mix together.
Adjust seasonings if necessary. Cover and simmer 30-40 minutes.
Cook spaghetti according to directions on package. Rinse and drain.
Keep spaghetti hot. Arrange spaghetti on hot serving platter and spoon sauce over it and sprinkle generously with grated Parmesan cheese. Or place hot spaghetti on individual plates, spoon over sauce and have a container of grated Parmesan cheese nearby so that each individual may serve himself.

6-8 servings

Mashed Potatoes and Ham Cakes

2 cups cold mashed potatoes
1 cup finely minced or ground cooked ham
Dash of Tabasco Sauce
½ tablespoon minced parsley
Flour or seasoned bread crumbs

Mix mashed potatoes and ham.
Add Worcestershire Sauce, parsley bits and hot sauce.
Shape mixture into ½" flat, firm, round cakes.
Cover with flour or fine buttered, seasoned bread crumbs.
Fry over medium heat; brown both sides of cake.
They can be fried in butter or bacon or sausage drippings.
Crisp sautéed bacon or sausage
may be substituted for the ham.
Yield 6-8 cakes

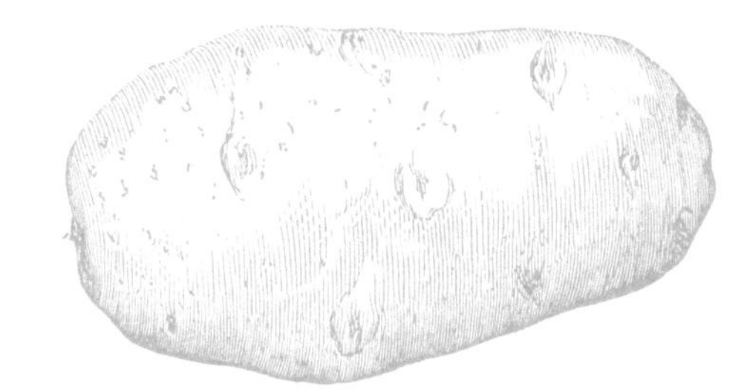

Quick and Easy Supper

1 cup converted rice
2 tablespoons butter or margarine
½ cup finely minced onion
1½ cups fully cooked ham, cut in small cubes
1¼ cups cream of mushroom soup
½ cup green peas or thinly sliced carrots
salt and pepper to taste
grated American or Parmesan cheese

Cook rice according to directions on package.
Add diced ham after rice begins to cook.
Sauté onions in the butter or margarine until they are well cooked but not browned. Add peas and/or carrots when rice is about done.
Add mushroom soup and salt and pepper to taste.
Let all simmer until rice is done. Stir several times during process.
Cook 45-50 minutes or until rice is done.
Add a bit of milk if it seems to be too dry.
Serve on a warmed platter.
Sprinkle lightly with either of the two cheeses.
It is very easy to prepare and quite filling.
A green salad on the side is very nice.
Serves 6-8

Potato Pancakes

6 medium-size potatoes
2 eggs
1½ tablespoons flour
¼ teaspoon baking powder
1¼ teaspoon salt
1½ teaspoon grated onion

Wash and peel potatoes. Soak potatoes in cold water for one hour.
Drain potatoes and dry them well. Grate potatoes on a coarse grater.
Drain them again and pat them with absorbent paper towels
to absorb any remaining liquid. Dry the grated onion as well.
There should be about 4 cups of grated potatoes.
Sift together the flour, baking powder and salt.
Mix flour, etc. with grated potatoes and onion.
Pour about ¼-inch of melted fat or oil into a deep skillet.
Make fat very hot. Test with a bit of the batter.
When hot enough, drop batter by spoonfuls, three or four cakes
depending on size of skillet.
The cakes should not touch. Brown cakes on one side.
Turn and brown on other side.
Remove from hot fat and drain on paper towels
on large platter or tray. Continue process until all batter is used.
Serve immediately. You may wish to make only one half of the recipe
if you have only two or three persons for the meal.
Well seasoned (sugar and cinnamon) applesauce
goes well with the potato pancakes.

Hominy and Brown Gravy

1 (20-ounce) can hominy
⅔ cup water
½ stick butter or margarine
1 tablespoon minced onion or onion flakes (optional)
6 slices bacon or ½ pound seasoned pork sausage
3 tablespoons bacon or sausage drippings
4 tablespoons flour
1½ cups hot milk or half and half
Salt and pepper to taste

Add ⅔ cup water to hominy.
Add butter and onions or onion flakes if desired.
Cover and place over medium heat to steam.
Cut bacon into ½-inch pieces. Place in skillet and sauté until crisp.
Set crisp bacon aside in warm place.
If using sausage, sauté until nicely browned.
Remove from skillet and set in warm place.
Spoon off drippings from skillet, leaving about three tablespoons in skillet. Add flour to remaining drippings in skillet.
Stir until lightly browned. Slowly add hot milk or half and half.
Stir and cook over moderate heat until a nice gravy has formed.
Season with salt and pepper to taste.
Add a bit more liquid if gravy is too thick.
Mix together the steamed hominy and sautéed bacon or sausage.
To serve, put hot hominy and meat in one bowl and hot gravy in gravy boat or bowl. Place serving spoon by hominy dish and small ladle for gravy boat or bowl so that gravy may be ladled over steamed hominy and meat.
If served at luncheon or dinner, buttered peas are good with this dish.
For breakfast, a dish of applesauce seasoned with ground cinnamon and sugar is ideal.
Serves 4-6

Slippery Pot Pie

6 pieces chicken, legs, thighs and breasts
2 medium-size potatoes, cooked
¾ cup minced celery
½ cup minced onion
½ cup sliced carrots or green peas
Pot pie pastry (see page 207)

Cook chicken in lightly salted water. When done, remove from pot.
Cook potatoes in lightly salted water.
Set aside chicken broth and potato broth also
as it might be needed to add to chicken broth.
When chicken and potatoes are cool enough to handle,
cut chicken into small pieces and dice potatoes.
Place chicken and potatoes into reserved chicken broth.
Add celery and other vegetables. Add some potato broth if needed.
The chicken and vegetables need to be well covered.
Bring to boil again. Add a bit more broth
and potato broth if necessary. Drop prepared pastry into
boiling liquid, one piece at a time.
Cover with tight lid and cook over slow heat about 10 minutes.
This recipe may be made with ham and ham broth.
This recipe is often made and served
at church suppers in our area.
Serves 6-8

Pot Pie Pastry

1 cup flour
1 tablespoon shortening
½ teaspoon baking powder
¼ teaspoon salt
2-3 tablespoons ice water or enough to moisten dough enough to roll into pastry

Mix ingredients as you would for pie dough.
Turn onto floured board. Roll to about 1/8" or less thickness.
Cut into rectangles or squares about 2-2½" in length.
Drop pastry piece by piece into boiling broth.
Cover well, reduce heat to slow boil
and cook about 10 minutes.

Vegetarian Quiche

8 ounces finely shredded Swiss cheese
1 cup small fresh mushrooms, sliced
½ cup finely sliced green spring onions
½ cup finely diced sweet green pepper
½ cup fresh or cooked tomatoes, diced
Sprinkle of sugar
¾ teaspoon salt
4 eggs
1 cup cream or half and half
½ teaspoon salt and ½ teaspoon garlic salt
1 tablespoon finely minced parsley
Dash or two Tabasco sauce
1 prepared pastry shell

Prepare and cover bottom of deep 9″ pie pan with pastry.
Prick bottom and sides of pastry shell. Crimp edges.
Bake shell in 450 degree oven for 10 minutes or until golden.
Remove from oven and set aside to cool.
Cover bottom of cooled shell with ½ of the shredded cheese.
Spread mushrooms over cheese.
Follow with onions and green pepper.
Spread tomatoes over pepper and onion.
Sprinkle a bit of sugar over tomatoes.
Beat eggs 1 or 2 minutes in mixer.
Add cream or half and half, both kinds of salt,
Tabasco sauce and minced parsley.
Pour liquid mix over ingredients in pie pan.
Spread remaining cheese over all in pie pan.
Bake in 350 degree oven 40-45 minutes.
Test with knife blade inserted into quiche.
The quiche is done if knife comes out clean.
If not, bake a few more minutes. Serve hot.
6 servings

Desserts

Apple Dessert

3 apples peeled and sliced in thick slices
½ cup sugar
2 cups warm water
2 tablespoons flour
½ cup seedless raisins
Dash salt
Melted butter
Ground nutmeg or cinnamon

Mix sugar, warm water, flour and salt together.
Arrange apple slices in two layers in lightly buttered baking dish.
Scatter raisins over apple slices over each layer.
Pour sugar, water, flour liquid over apples and raisins.
Sprinkle nutmeg or cinnamon lightly over casserole.
Drizzle melted butter over apples, etc.
Bake in 350° oven 30-45 minutes until apples are done.
This is a versatile dish.
It may be served hot in winter along with pork or
other meat dishes and in summer, cold, with whipped cream
or ice cream as a dessert.
Serves 4-6

Fruit Soufflé

1½ cups canned peach slices, diced
½ cup crushed pineapple
3 tablespoons melted butter
4 tablespoons flour
¼ teaspoon salt
1 cup milk
4 eggs, separated
4 tablespoons sugar
1 teaspoon vanilla

Spoon diced peaches and pineapple into lightly buttered casserole. Beat egg yolks until thick, adding sugar gradually. Set aside. Blend together butter, flour and salt in saucepan. Slowly add milk and cook and stir constantly until it thickens. Add beaten egg yolks and sugar, a little at a time, until well blended. Set aside to cool. When mixture is about lukewarm, add vanilla and mix all with fruit in casserole. Beat egg whites until they form soft peaks, but are not dry. Fold into mixture in casserole until all are nicely combined. Set filled casserole into a shallow pan filled with hot water about an inch or so deep. Place in 350° oven and bake about 40-45 minutes or until soufflé is set. This dish is good served as a dessert with cold milk, whipped cream or ice cream. Other fruits may be used instead of peaches and pineapple. Canned sweet white cherries, apricots, or mandarin oranges. Serves 6

Easy Peach Cobbler

1 cup sugar
½ cup flour
1 cup milk
½ cup butter (1 stick)
1 (29-ounce) can sliced peaches (diced)
Pastry for single-crust pie

Mix and blend together sugar, flour and milk.
Melt butter in 1½ quart baking dish.
Pour flour, sugar, milk mixture into baking dish.
Spoon peaches over top of mixture. Do not stir. Top with pastry.
Make several slashes in pastry to allow steam to escape.
Brush pastry with milk.
Place baking dish into 400 degree preheated oven.
Bake 25-30 minutes or until pastry top is a golden brown.
Serves 8-9

Sweet Pastry

1½ cups flour
1 teaspoon baking powder
½ teaspoon salt
2 tablespoons sugar
½ cup shortening
4 tablespoons water
1 beaten egg yolk

Sift together flour, baking powder, salt and sugar.
Mix together shortening and flour mixture.
Stir in beaten egg yolk and water.
Stir quickly and form into a soft ball. Chill in refrigerator.
Roll out pastry on floured board to about ⅛ inch.
Line pie pan with pastry. Crimp edges.
Prick bottom and sides of shell with fork.
Bake in 425 degree oven 10-15 minutes of until lightly browned.
This pastry is excellent for any open-faced pie.
Yield 1 shell

The pastry may also be used for pies that are lined with unbaked pastry, filled and then baked.
Any leftover pastry may be cut into diamond or round shapes, placed over pie filling and baked in the usual way.

Fruit in Watermelon Shell

1 seedless watermelon
1 cantaloupe
1 honeydew melon
1 box strawberries
1 or 2 heads or bunches of leaf lettuce
Nectarines, grapes or strawberries for garnish

Wash and dry melons. Cut about 1½" slice off top of watermelon.
Cut as evenly as possible around top of melon.
With melon baller, remove bulk of melon from both
the top slice and lower part of melon.
After removing as much of the melon as possible,
scrape rest of pink melon with tablespoon and
remove from melon shell. Turn shell upside down and drain.
Proceed to make a saw-tooth edge around melon.
Cut about ½" diagonally forming a saw-tooth edge.
Drain shell again. Remove melon balls from cantaloupe and
honeydew. Drain again. Make a bed of lettuce on large tray.
Position shell on lettuce in center of tray.
Fill shell with fruit, alternating watermelon, cantaloupe
and honeydew melon balls.
Slice a few of the strawberries and scatter between layers of melon.
Save some of the strawberries for garnish on top of melon,
alternating the berries with honeydew balls.
Garnish base of melon shell with nectarines,
strawberries and/or grapes.
Leftover fruit may be used to refill shell or enjoy later.

Fruit Bowl or Tray

Just as attractive as the melon-filled shell, and
if preparation time is a concern, you may wish to prepare
a lovely fruit-filled bowl instead.
A punch bowl or large, relatively shallow glass dish
are quite attractive filled with fruit.
Using the same variety of fruits and melons, layer the prepared fruit,
balls or cubed, in the bowl or dish.
Garnish with sliced apples, strawberries, mandarin
or orange slices around edge of bowl.
Arrange strawberry halves or apple slices in center of filled fruit.
Chill until serving time.

Just as eye catching is a lovely fruit tray.
Layer tray with washed, patted dry leaf lettuce or other lettuce.
Cut various melons into ½″ cubes.
Pineapple chunks are showy to put in center of tray.
Arrange other melon, perhaps watermelon, on each end of tray.
Alternate sections of cubed cantaloupe
and honeydew on sides of tray.
Use red apple slices or strawberries as dividers
of the various sections of fruit. Chill until serving time.
Most any way you wish to arrange the various fruits
is beautiful and has great eye appeal.
Servings depend on quantities of fruit used.

(see photo page 164)

We are all God's children,

so be kind to one another,

for everyone is either friend, sister or brother.

Miscellaneous

Uses for Leftover Foods

What do you do with leftover foods? Many families do not like to be served leftover food, particularly if the same dish has been presented to them several times. Food is so expensive, it pays to save it and offer it to the family in other guises. Most cooked foods can be refrigerated or frozen and used in recipes you may prepare at a later date. For instance, soups are an excellent way to use many of the leftovers. Soups do not require a large quantity of any one ingredient.

Leftover vegetables

green beans	tomatoes
green peas	broccoli
creamed or baked corn	cauliflower
carrots	potatoes

All of the above vegetables can be used in soups, chowders, stews, sauces or casseroles.

Leftover Rice etc.

rice, white and brown	noodles
hominy	macaroni
pearl barley	spaghetti

These foods can also be used in soups, casseroles and as a filler in different dishes

Leftover Meats, Fish and Poultry

chicken	salmon
turkey	tuna
beef roast	baked fish
pork roast	lamb

All of the above are excellent in soups, stews, bisques, chowders, and fish cakes, etc.

Leftover Fruits

peaches	apples
pears	prunes
pineapple	grapes

These fruits, whether fresh or cooked, can be used in salads, pies, parfaits, or hot fruit casseroles

Leftover breads and cakes

biscuits	coffee cakes
rolls	cookies
muffins	fruit breads

These items can be reheated, dried and crumbled, cubed for fillings for poultry or fish, they can become crumbs for your casseroles. Crumbled they can be used as topping for parfaits or garnishes for icecream or fruit desserts. If you can save and use them at a later date, they may help you out in an emergency as well, by saving you a quick impromptu trip to the grocer's.

Grilled Cheese Sandwich

Easily made sandwich for a quick lunch on a busy day.

2 slices white or whole wheat bread
2 tablespoons butter or margarine
1 large or 2 small slices American or sharp cheddar cheese

If a griddle is not available, the sandwich can be made in a skillet.
Melt half the butter in the skillet over moderate heat.
Spread the other half of the butter on one slice of bread.
You may use a bit more butter if you like.
The cheese should be about ⅛ inch thick.
Place it between the two unbuttered sides of the bread slices.
Place unbuttered slice of sandwich onto the melted butter in the pan.
Grill a few minutes until the under slice seems to be browning.
Turn sandwich over on buttered side and grill until cheese
seems to have melted and bread is browned.
Remove from heat. Cut in half and enjoy.
A bowl of hot cream of tomato soup along with the grilled cheese
sandwich makes for a very satisfying light lunch.

Stewed Apples and Raisins

2½ cups water
½ to 1 cup sugar, depending on tartness of apples
¼ teaspoon salt
4 cups pared or unpared apples (remove core)
¾ cup seedless raisins

Slice or dice apples. Boil together water, sugar, and salt until a light syrup is formed. Add apples and raisins to syrup. Simmer until tender. Remove from heat, cool, and refrigerate.
6-8 servings.

***These are excellent as a side dish for fried or roasted meats. They can be simmered in a lighter syrup. An excellent snack for children after they return home from school.*

Fried Apples

4-6 tart apples
4 tablespoons butter
½ cup white or light-brown sugar (packed)
¼ teaspoon cinnamon

Mix sugar and cinnamon. Slice and core apples.
Melt butter in skillet. Add apples, sauté, and turn them
so they may brown slightly and not burn.
When lightly browned on all sides, add a little more butter
if you think it necessary.
Sprinkle the apples with the mixed sugar
and add a bit more if you think the apples are quite tart.
Reduce heat and cover with a tight lid.
Let the apples simmer until they are tender.

***This dish is excellent served with a pork or beef roast.*
Gala apples are good served this way.
Bacon drippings may be substituted for the butter.

Puddin' and Hominy

1 pound country pork puddin'
1 28-oz can hominy
1 tablespoon melted butter
¼ cup water

Toss hominy, butter and water together.
Place in pan with a tight lid and allow hominy
to steam over a low heat.
Place puddin' in a small pan or skillet over low heat
and allow it to heat through until hot.
Quite a bit of fat will have become liquid.
Pour fat into a side container.
You may lift puddin' with a large slotted spoon
and place in a large sieve to drain.
When well drained, return it to pan and cover until it is again hot.
Put hot steamed hominy in one serving disk
and the hot puddin' in another.
Family can serve themselves and mix quantities
of each dish as they please.
The puddin' is very, very rich, but eaten with hominy it is very good.
Applesauce, apple butter, or fried apples
are a nice side dish.

**This has been a staple for farm families over the years,*
especially during the cold winter months.
Particularly by the farmers who did their own butchering.

Hot Chocolate

1½ blocks semi-sweet chocolate
¼ cup sugar
¼ teaspoon salt
1 cup boiling water
3 cups scalded milk
½ teaspoon vanilla
sweetened whipped cream, melted marshmallows or whipped topping

Melt chocolate in small sauce pan in warm oven,
or low burner on stove.
When melted add sugar, salt and boiling water.
Stir and blend until chocolate is completely melted.
Stir chocolate mix into scalded milk.
Stir and blend well, add vanilla. Pour into cups.
Top with melted marshmallows or a dollop of sweetened
whipped cream or whipped topping.
A real treat at the end of a cold day.
Serves 4

Rhubarb Sauce

This is an old, old recipe when most of us grew our own rhubarb.

Wash and "skin" rhubarb if necessary.
Cut ribs into one-inch pieces.
Cover with 2 cups sugar to 4 cups (1 quart) rhubarb.
Add just enough water to melt the sugar.
Let it set for an hour or so.
Cook over medium heat and stir occasionally
until rhubarb is tender and has become a nice sauce.
Serve cold. It is delicious served with lightly sweetened
whipped cream. It may also be spooned over cake or ice cream.
Four cups rhubarb will make about four cups of sauce.

Watermelon Pickle

1 pound watermelon rind
1 cup salt
4 cups water

SYRUP
1 cup water
1 cup vinegar
2 cups sugar
1 (3-inch) stick cinnamon
8 whole cloves, heads removed
Orange and lemon rind (optional)

To prepare watermelon rind, cut away outside rind
and remaining pink melon meat. Cut the rind into ½-inch cubes.
Rinse, drain and weigh rind.
Allowing 1 cup salt and 4 cups water to each pound of rind,
cover and soak rind overnight or about 12 hours.
Rinse, drain and rinse again.
Cover again with water and slowly boil about 10 minutes
or until rind is half tender. Drain and set aside.
In saucepan, mix together cup of vinegar, cup of water,
sugar, spices (that have been tied securely in a bag), and the lemon
and orange rind if using. Bring all to a boil.
Then simmer until a nice medium to thick syrup forms.
Add melon rind and bring to boil, cut heat and just simmer,
do not boil, about 10 minutes.
Remove spice bag and orange and lemon rinds.
Pack pickle in sterilized jars. Cover with hot syrup and seal with lids.
Store in cool place. This is an old, old recipe but worth the effort.
Quantities depend on quantities of rind.
About 2½ cups per pound of rind.

Squash Casserole

5 lbs. yellow squash
1 large onion, chopped
2 red peppers, chopped
2 cans diced water chestnuts
¼ teaspoon pepper
2 tablespoons olive oil
½ cup mayonnaise
1½ cups sharp Cheddar cheese
1 egg, beaten
2 tablespoons butter
¼ cup dry plain bread crumbs.

Slice and boil squash until tender. Drain and set aside.
Sauté onion and red peppers in olive oil until tender.
Mix together water chestnuts, squash, red pepper and onion mixture, pepper, mayonnaise, cheese, and egg.
Pour into a 2 quart casserole dish. Heat butter in a small fry pan.
Add dry bread crumbs to melted butter and toast lightly.
Sprinkle over squash mixture.
Bake in preheated oven at 350° for 30 minutes.
May be made ahead of time and refrigerated overnight.

GRAND-DAUGHTER, DIANE KIMBLE

Party Rolls

For a small or large dinner party, this recipe
added to Mother's famous rolls will bring you compliments.

Using Mother's recipe, when you make your rolls, shape them
in a muffin tin, 3 formed balls to a section, to form a cloverleaf.
This makes a fancier shape for your party and is a sweeter roll
than many which allows such a wonderful end product.

Rum Flavored Icing Topping (or orange flavoring may be used)

¾ cup + 1 tablespoon confectionary sugar (more or less to desired consistency)
1 tablespoon milk, half & half or cream
½ teaspoon rum (or orange) flavoring

Place confectionary sugar in a bowl.
Stir to smooth. Add milk, half & half or cream.
Add flavoring to measure or to taste.
When rolls are pulled warm from the oven,
using a pastry brush or other item you desire,
spread icing over top of rolls and place
in your container of choice.

DAUGHTER, PATRICIA FERRELL

Joan's Zucchini Bread

3 large eggs
2 cups granulated sugar
1 cup Crisco oil
3 cups flour
1 teaspoon baking soda
1 teaspoon baking powder
1 teaspoon salt
1 teaspoon ground cinnamon
2 teaspoons vanilla
¾ cup chopped nuts
¾ cup flaked coconut
3 cups grated raw zucchini

Sift together flour, baking soda, baking powder, salt and cinnamon. In mixer, beat eggs, add sugar slowly. Add oil and mix well. Gradually add flour mixture a little at a time until all has been added. Add vanilla. Fold into the mixture the nuts, coconut and zucchini. Blend well. Pour in loaf pans.
Bake in 350 degree oven 45-60 minutes depending on size of pans, 3-4 pans.

DAUGHTER, JOAN DERRICK

Ice Box Cookies

1 pound oleo (margarine)
1 cup granulated sugar
1 cup light-brown sugar (packed)
2 eggs, beaten
1 teaspoon baking soda
6 cups sifted flour
1 cup chopped nuts
2 teaspoons ground cinnamon

Sift together flour and baking soda.
Cream oleo well. Add sugars gradually beating well
until mixture is light and fluffy. Beat in eggs.
Add dry ingredients slowly. Fold in nuts.
Divide and form dough into rolls about 1¾ inches in diameter
(smaller or larger as you choose).
Refrigerate until well chilled.
Cut in slices and bake in 350 degree oven.
This recipe makes about 100 cookies.

It is an old, old recipe handed down
through the Derrick family.

DAUGHTER, JOAN DERRICK

Best-Ever Meat Loaf

⅓ cup oatmeal
1 cup milk
1½ lbs. lean ground beef
2 eggs, beaten to mix
1 medium onion
1 garlic clove, chopped
3/4 teaspoon salt
½ teaspoon fresh or dried sage, chopped
Pepper to taste

TOPPING:
1 cup ketchup
1 tablespoon Dijon mustard

Preheat oven to 350 degrees.
Soak the oatmeal in the milk for 5 minutes.
Add rest of ingredients. Mix well. Place in 9-inch loaf pan.

Top with half of the topping. Bake for two hours.
Add the rest of the sauce for the last 10 minutes.

GRAND-DAUGHTER, DEBORAH BISSELL

Recipes for Living a Contented Life

Always remember that life is a gift to you - How you deal with it is a duly challenge and blessing.

Try to take each day with a deep breath and take each problem, challenge, and changes as best you can.
There is sometimes not immediate answers to everything we face.
Pray for patience and guidance for each day - and always look for a more peaceful tomorrow.
Have patience with others and put yourselves in the shoes of others - Big help - that will get you thru many a day.
Love each other & always care for the young - disabled & our eldery.
love Mom 11/8/20

Recipes for Living a Contented Life

We can live a joyous life if we learn to concentrate on the good,
the beautiful, the happy times we experience day by day.

Weep not over yesterday and what might have been,
but rejoice in today and look forward with hope and faith
for tomorrow and whatever it may bring.

Never resist an urge to do a kind deed.
I believe these impulses are God-given.
That opportunity to do good may never come to us again.

Learning to count our blessings instead of our disappointments
can go a long way in giving us a happier outlook on life.

To dream is wonderful, but to work toward
and accomplish that dream is a joy indeed.

We should never borrow trouble from tomorrow. Many times
the things we are most concerned about never come to pass.

Each day of our life is a precious gift.
Use it well. Be thankful for it and rejoice in it.

When our little ones say or do some funny, loving, sweet or brilliant little thing, we should write it down. Years later the memories will be sweet and bring a smile to your face, sometimes even a tear; precious, precious memories of days long ago. You may want to share them with your now grown children.

When your spouse does something especially kind or loving for you, make a note of it. Years later you may share that special memory and what it meant to you at the time.

A child, like yours and mine is like a beautiful flower. To grow to his or her full potential, needs the sunshine of love, the refreshing water of knowledge, and the warmth of a nurturing environment.

If we would really count our blessings, we might not be so prone to concentrate on the disappointments in our life.

I am confident we human beings live our lives more in our mind and spirit than we do in our body. The mind and spirit are the motivators that lead and direct us on the paths we ultimately take in life.

One who thinks he has never made a mistake in life has really never done too much in his or her life.
Sometimes our mistakes are really stepping stones to wisdom.

A kind or encouraging word given to a friend or brother in his time of trial may lift him from the brink of utter despair. Be there for him.

They say we get many more wrinkles when frowning than we do when smiling. When smiling, we are much happier too.

Listen. We learn much more by listening than we do when controlling the conversation. Our own thoughts we already know.

A cheerful mind can only make our walk on the road of life
a joy day by day.

Hope and faith are that ray of sunshine to warm our hearts
and minds on our darkest days.

Make the most of each day, for this day, today, is special.
It is one day among many that make up what we call our life.

It's a good thing to remember-there is really no point in
crying over spilled milk!

Hope and prayer can be a real life-line between
utter despair and inner peace.

One is never really, really old, until he thinks he is.

Life is what we make it. Let's make it the very best we can.

There is a time to press forward and a time to be patient.
Fortunate are we when we know the difference.

My Journey

I have had a long, long journey in this life of mine.
I can only marvel, how quickly has gone by the time.
I have climbed life's highest mountains,
and forged deep treacherous streams.
I have cried my private tears and dreamed my secret dreams.
I have known my share of happiness and deepest sorrow, too.
But through the ups and downs of life, God has seen me through.
I have let my mind take me, to all the wonderful places,
I couldn't go in reality, and I have traveled these
many, many places by land and air and sea.

I have borne my children and watched them grow
into some of the nicest people I'll ever know.
I have lived to see grandchildren, great-grandchildren,
and great-great-grandchildren too, I hope to see.
May God bless them each one, these, my life's legacy.
I have loved, and been loved, and am loved, this I know.
For in so many ways, family and friends let it show.

I have been content in whatever situation or place
I found myself to be, knowing God was in charge of my life's Odyssey.
I always felt I was in the place He wanted me to be,
doing what I was doing, and doing it happily.
For God gave me the strength, the will, and the opportunity.

What more could any one ask of life than I have already been given?
My life's clock has long since struck eleven;
and now I look forward someday to a life of peace and joy,
with friends and loved ones, forever more,
at home, in heaven.

Life's little lessons along the way

are stepping stones to wisdom.